Physical Characteristics of the Border Collie
(from the American Kennel Club breed standard)

Topline: Back is level from behind the withers to the slightly arched, muscular loins, falling to a gently sloping croup.

Tail: Set on low and moderately long with the bone reaching at least to the hock. The ideal tail carriage is low when the dog is concentrating on a given task and may have a slight upward swirl at the end like a shepherd's crook.

Hindquarters: Broad and muscular, in profile sloping gracefully to the low set tail. The thighs are long, broad, deep and muscular. Stifles are well turned with strong hocks that may be either parallel or very slightly turned in. Dewclaws should be removed. Feet, although slightly smaller, are the same as front.

Coat: Two varieties are permissible, both having close-fitting, dense, weather resistant double coats with the top coat either straight or wavy and coarser in texture than the undercoat which is soft, short and dense.

Size: The height at the withers varies from 19 to 22 inches for males, 18 to 21 inches for females.

Color: All colors or combination of colors and/or markings.

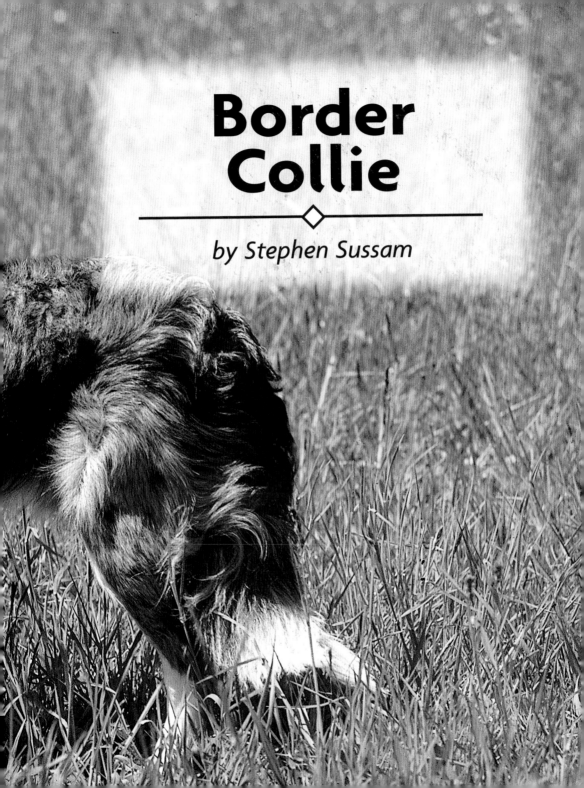

Border Collie

by Stephen Sussam

Contents

KENNEL CLUB BOOKS: **BORDER COLLIE**
ISBN: 1-59378-211-X

Copyright © 2005 • Kennel Club Books, LLC
308 Main Street, New Jersey 07711 USA
Cover Design Patented: US 6,435,559 B2 • Printed in South Korea

Photography by

Paulette Braun, T.J. Calhoun, Alan and Sandy Carey, Carolina Biological Supply, Kent and Donna Dannen, Isabelle Français, Carol Ann Johnson, Bill Jonas, Dr. Dennis Kunkel, Nancy Liguori, John S. Muzyka, Tam C. Nguyen, Phototake, Jean Claude Revy, Karen Taylor and C. James Webb.

Illustrations by Patricia Peters.

The Border Collie
has been called
the "most
intelligent dog in
the world." He can
be a wonderful
pet, guardian and
loyal friend.

HISTORY OF THE

BORDER COLLIE

Perhaps the Border Collie is not the most obvious choice of most pet owners given its fantastic reputation as a working sheepdog on fields in Great Britain and ranches in America. The breed's prowess in moving ornery flocks up and down hills is surely well known, as is its willingness to obey the shepherds. In our modern age, however, the Border Collie has gained new fame as "the most intelligent dog in the world," as certain popular dog books have acclaimed and the breed's accomplishments in the arenas of obedience and agility trials attest. For the pet owner, this intelligence and willingness to obey translate into a tractable and loyal companion dog.

It is human nature rather than animal nature that becomes a consideration in this discussion of the Border Collie. We have all seen the individual who chooses to drive the sleekest racing machine along the common thoroughfare to work and back, or perhaps the person who purchases the all-terrain technological triumph, a vehicle ready for the Indy 500, for the trip to school or the mall. To so under-employ such technology or expertise must be a factor of imagination or conspicuous display. Or perhaps admiration.

Let us agree that it is admiration and the love of so perfect and honorable a breed that compels

Admirers of the Border Collie do not live exclusively on ranches or farms. Today the handsome Border Collie attracts owners from coast to coast.

the new potential owner, who lives nowhere near a farm or ranch and whose business with sheep occurs only during sleepless nights to purchase and share his life with a Border Collie. Given the breed's original purpose, owning a Border Collie as a pet is, in the strictest sense, incorrect. The history, purpose and heart of the animal itself converge upon one utilitarian theme: work. This is a working dog, and those who choose it as a pet for whatever reasons of admiration, emulation or reverse snobbery must understand and accommodate its practical soul.

The ancient and necessary truce that first brought man and dog together is slightly outside our scope. The relevant point is that the working Border Collie evolved from early guarding and herding animals. Most writers call upon the 1570 *Treatise of Englishe Dogges* by Johannes Caius as the first printed reference to the working sheepdog:

"This dogge, either at the hearing of his master's voyce, or at the wagging and whisteling in his fist, or at his shrill and hoarse hissing bringeth the wandering weathers and straying sheepe into the self same place where his master's will and wishe is to have them, whereby the shepherd reapeth this benefite, namely, that with little labour and no toyle or moving of his feete he may rule

and guide his flocke, according to his owne desire, either to have them go forward, or to stand styll, or to drawe backward, or to turne this way to take that way. For it is not in Englande as it is in Fraunce, as it is in Flaunders, as it is in Syria, as it is in Tartaria, where the sheepe follow the shepherd, for heere in our country, the shepherd followeth the sheepe. And sometimes the straying sheepe, when no dogge runneth before them, gather themselves together in a flocke when they hear the shepherd whistel in his fist, for feare of the dogge (as I imagine) remembering this (if unreasonable creatures may be reported to have memory) that the dogge commonly runneth out at his master's warrant which is his whistel. This have we often times diligently marcked in taking our journey from towne to towne. When we have heard a shepherd whistel, we have rayned in our horse and stood styll a space to see the proofe and trial of this matter. Furthermore with this dogge doth the shepherd take the sheepe for ye slaughter and to be healed if they be sicke, no hurt or harme in the world done to the simple creature."

Although the appearance of the dog is not described here, the performance is that of the modern Border Collie. The essence of that performance has not changed for hundreds of years, and in regard to sheep herding, neither has the Border Collie. Skills have been refined and perfected as prized workers were selectively bred and sold. Appearance, although never a true concern of breeders and owners of this working dog, changed little since 1790 when a woodcut in *Bewick's History of Quadrapeds* depicted a shepherd's dog that bears a pronounced resemblance to today's Border Collie.

The Rough Collie, sometimes called the Scotch Collie, is closely related to the Border Collie. It is a more substantial dog with an abundant double coat.

Of course, a shepherd's dog, a sheepdog, is any dog that works with sheep and not necessarily a "collie." Although the origin and exact meaning of the name remains unknown, some contend that it comes from the word *coley*, denoting black; others say it comes from the Welsh word *coelius*, meaning faithful; while still others claim that the name comes from *colley*, referring to a Scottish type of sheep. The designation "Border" is easier to trace, describing the areas where the dogs were prominently used, the Scottish border of England.

KING OF THE HILL

While many farmers have attempted to replace their dogs with mechanical devices, most have failed miserably! As any shepherd will confirm, a good Border Collie is worth his weight in platinum! The Collies that work in the hill country have the most difficult of tasks and terrain. Neither tractors nor motor bikes can maneuver over rocks, hills and streams, where the Border Collie is called upon to cast out the hill sheep, which are about as light and agile as the Collie himself.

The English Shepherd is an American spin-off of the Border Collie. Not widely known in its homeland, the English Shepherd is primarily a stockdog.

BEYOND THE SHEEP AND COWS

The Border Collie has been offered employment on a variety of livestock beyond the usual ovine and bovine types. Reports of Border Collies as poultry pushers, working successfully with geese, chickens, turkeys and ducks, have stared "down" many feathers. Some Collies have even ruffled the ostrich's feathers. Of the four-legged varieties, the Border Collie has stared down the likes of buffalo, emu, goats, pigs, alpaca, rhea, fallows and sitka deer. Given the breed's talents, this roster could one day be as lengthy as Noah's!

Today there are five popular incarnations of the collie, each regarded as a separate breed: the Rough Collie, the Smooth Collie, the Shetland Sheepdog, the Bearded Collie and the Border Collie. The popularity of these breeds with the British people began with the favor bestowed upon them by Queen Victoria, who owned several. An 1860 portrait of one of her dogs, Gypsie, shows us a mostly black animal who today would be taken for a pure-bred Border Collie. Although the Rough Collie was more commonly seen in artwork, it can be inferred that the Border Collie was the original type from which the more elegant breeds were developed. These Rough Collies were bred taller, with more emphasis upon a full coat, longer, narrower heads and refined color.

The Australian Shepherd is American, not Australian, despite its name. Approximately the same size as the Border Collie, the Aussie is squarer, heavier coated and slightly taller.

In addition, there are many other types of herding dogs in the world bred from Border Collie stock, including the Australian Kelpie and the American cousins: the Australian Shepherd, the Farm Collie, the English Shepherd and the McNab. The histories of these colonial relatives are as

Doing what he does best, this Border Collie shows the intensity and love of work that make the breed singularly exceptional.

similar to the Border Collie as are their looks and characteristics. All are working stockdogs and were imported into the US and Australia during the late 19th century along with the Scots and the sheep who began the vast

NIPPING THE BOVINE

Barking and baying at sleeping cows is no pastime for the quick-minded Border Collie. While many of the traditional cattle dogs, such as the Bouvier des Flandres and the Australian Cattle Dog, stir their cows by barking, the Border Collie is a quiet worker that moves the cows by nipping at their feet. The cows often try to kick the dogs, but the Collie's low stance keeps them out of hooves' way.

sheep ranches. Many of these working animals were not registered because many farmers never bothered with such matters and the dogs' ancestors arrived before there was a registry in England.

The Border Collie, not molded to a particular physical standard, continued to be bred for work and work alone. While modern Border Collies can all be traced to a few distinguished forebears, other breeds have been introduced from time to time with the aim of improving working performance. In fact, the most famous characteristic of the Border Collie, the power of the eye to control stock, was bred into the breed from gundogs like setters, pointers and spaniels. James Hogg, the Scottish shepherd poet, wrote in 1790 a

The Shetland Sheepdog, a close relation of the Border Collie, is a miniature version of the Rough Collie. He stands only two-thirds the height of the Border Collie.

description of a dog showing "eye" which is applicable to any Border Collie today:

"Whenever the dog was within doors, his whole occupation was watching and pointing the cat from morning to night. When she flitted from one place to another, so did he in a moment; and then squatting down, he kept his point sedulously till he was either called off or fell asleep."

The Border Collie's farm work necessitates that he be able to work with all types of animals.

SEE AMERICA'S FIVE!
Although the United States has originated comparatively few of its own breeds of dog, breeders have yielded five interesting sheepdogs, all cousins to the Border Collie. The only breed to be fully recognized by the American Kennel Club is our "first cousin," the Australian Shepherd. The Aussie, as he is often called, standing 18 to 23 inches, is a handsome symmetrical tailless stock dog with an elegant medium-length coat. The English Shepherd is a stockier, squarer dog than the Border Collie, from which it derives. These lesser known sheepdogs developed in the Midwest and East and are nearly identical to the Farm Collie. The Farm Collies are merely crosses of Border Collies imported into the US used for various types of farm and ranch work. The McNab, named for its importer Alexander McNab of California, is a medium-built dog with a smooth coat and prick ears. Like the Border Collie, it is usually black and white. The Basque Shepherd is a direct descendant of the Australian Shepherd, appearing identical except that he maintains his tail! Unlike his tailless brother, he is not recognized by the AKC.

A related result of this early crossbreeding with gundogs is the well-developed scenting ability and retrieving instincts of Border Collies. These abilities are made good use of in obedience trials but are sometimes a problem for dogs that are tempted away from work at the scent of a rabbit.

The International Sheep Dog Society (ISDS) was created in

In the UK and US, the Border Collie has enjoyed a winning reputation in the show ring as well as in trials and on farms.

1906. These early owners and handlers set out to protect and improve the breed through working trials and a registry. A stud book was first compiled in 1951, listing over 14,000 dogs. The book has grown by over 6,000 registrations each year since then. A common entry in the stud book would show the influence of the bloodlines created by J. M. Wilson, the most renowned Border Collie breeder and handler of all time. His Whitehope dogs are the basis of many modern pedigrees.

THE BORDER COLLIE IN AMERICA

Although the Border Collie ranks as one of the most popular breeds in Britain, the breed has gained a considerable following in the United States as well. Since the 19th century, when Americans

A COLLIE BY ANY OTHER COLOR...

In England and Ireland, the Border Collie is a black and white affair. In the US, however, where the diversity

of the "Rainbow" persistently shines, other colors are beginning to become commonplace. The once rare chocolate or liver has become popular. Other colors that can be spotted on Border Collies include: silver (black with white speckling), blue merle, slate gray (or blue), sable, lemon (yellow), ginger (red), fawn (a dilute liver) and brindle (combination of brown and black). Let's not forget that solid white Border Collies are not frowned upon in the US as they are in the UK.

Not known primarily as a show dog, the Border Collie fends well in conformation, as evidenced by this handsome winner and his rightly proud young owner.

Nevertheless, by the 1920s and 1930s, trials were held around the US, not only in the West but in the Midwest and East as well. Small trials were held as a part of agricultural fairs, and larger trials sponsored by the sheepdog registries became well known in working-dog circles. In recent times, the United States Border Collie Handlers Association (USBCHA), formed in 1979, exists to regulate the way trials in the US are held. The organization also sponsors two annual trials, and the winners of these trials are held in very high esteem.

A number of ranchers maintained their own private registries (for their own dogs); McClain, Perrot and Topliff are examples of early registries. The North American Sheep Dog Society (NASDS) began registering Border Collies in 1940. Prior to this, dogs were registered with the British registry, ISDS, which remains an affiliate of most major registries today. James Reid along with his fellow ranchers, sheepdog handlers and enthusiasts founded the new American organization. About a decade later, in 1952, the American International Border Collie Registry was founded by a band of disgruntled NASDS folk from Iowa. Today both registries continue to function and promote the breed and its working ability.

The American Border Collie Association (ABCA), founded in

were expanding westward, the Border Collie secured an important place in US history. The California Gold Rush drew thousands of pioneers westward and their sheepdogs accompanied them, moving cattle and sheep and protecting their livestock. The wide expanses of land attracted sheep ranchers and cattle farmers, and experienced Scottish, Spanish and English shepherds brought over dogs. Many of them were Border Collies.

Sheepdog trials, which enjoy a large cultural following in Britain, have never caught on with great intensity in the US.

1983, was the third registry to be formed and became the most active registry, with over 9,000 members. They can be contacted on the Internet at www.american-bordercollie.org.

The Border Collie might be considered lucky to have so many parent clubs, though the situation involving the breed's three parent clubs does somewhat resemble a never-ending divorce and custody trial. Among the parent clubs are the Border Collie Society of America (BSCA), the American Border Collie Alliance (ABCA) and the United States Border Collie Club (USBCC), the latter of which strongly opposed the breed's entrance into the ranks of the American Kennel Club (AKC). The USBCC, founded in 1975 to prevent the breed's becoming a "show dog," promoted the breed's working ability and participation in obedience trials.

The breed's involvement with AKC dates back to the 1930s when the Border Collie began competing in obedience trials. When the Miscellaneous Class was formed in 1955, the Border Collie was one of its inaugural members. The breed remained in the Miscellaneous Class (whose members are denied championship status) for four decades, enjoying its admittance into obedience trials but rarely competing in conformation shows. In a controversial decision,

AKC accepted the Border Collie into the Herding Group as its 139th breed, effective February 1, 1995. AKC acceptance also indicates that the breed is registered with the organization as well. The AKC accepts Border Collies registered with the American Border Collie Association, the American International Border Collie Registry and the North American Sheepdog Society.

Although hundreds of Border Collies compete in AKC show rings every year, the breed's accomplishments and reputation in the performance trials are much more impressive, including the top Obedience Trial Champion of all time, OTCh. Heelalong Chimney Sweep, owned by D. and K. Guetzloff, and numerous other top obedience, agility and herding titlists.

THE EYES HAVE IT!

Border Collies possess a unique working trait in their ability to move stock with just their eyes. This ability to "stare down" the sheep in order to move them is called "strong eye" and is believed to be inherited from crosses to gundogs years ago. While some herding dogs bark, circle and nip to move their woolly charges, the Border Collie merely uses its unswerving stare to move the flock along.

BORDER COLLIE

A Border Collie's work is not limited to sheep; they often work with cattle as well.

The Border Collie's character is entirely related to the breed's occupation and purpose. While this holds special relevance to the owner of working Border Collies, the pet owner can appreciate these long-developed characteristics of the working dog and will see evidence of these herding instincts in his pet. In many cases it would require specific training

to fully revive and solidify these instincts, but understanding the dog's background gives the pet owner insight into his Border Collie's behavior, personality and natural aptitudes. Let's discuss the unique terms that are used in defining the Border Collie's traits and working ability.

THE BORDER COLLIE DEFINED
OUTRUN
The Border Collie must not simply chase sheep but must also be able to turn and direct them. The dog does not travel in straight lines, but runs out wide to gather the sheep. The dog who lacks an instinctual cast, or turning ability, will cut in too close to the sheep, merely startling them, not gathering them. A dog with a good outrun will naturally know how

---

STAR QUALITY
The inborn qualities of a top Border Collie must include:

- A natural cast or outrun
- Sufficient eye to gather and control sheep
- Power enough to face down and direct a single sheep without rushing or biting
- Intelligence, which allows him to take the initiative when necessary
- Temperament amenable to training and occasional correction without sulking, snarling or running away
- A strong constitution

"Eye" is a unique quality of the Border Collie. This dog approaches the sheep with the characteristic stare and his head held low.

to keep the proper distance between himself and the sheep.

Eye

Eye is one of the most unique qualities of the Border Collie and the most interesting instinct that you may observe in your pet. It is an attribute that has taken many generations to breed into the animal. Eye is a mesmerizing gaze that the dog levels at sheep, holding them in position. The Border Collie's stance is rigid, with the body and head held low, roughly similar to a gundog as it points. This ability, in fact, may have been added to the Border Collie from breeding with hunting dogs. Strong-eyed dogs can hold a small flock of sheep in the open with little running about.

Power

Power is the rather undefinable ability of the top dog to domi-

---

A BORDER COLLIE'S WORK IS NEVER DONE

The usual and rightful occupation for the Border Collie is farm work. Here these silent working and strong-eyed dogs are employed in several categories of work, which may be described as:

• work with sheep on hills
• work with lowland sheep
• work with dairy cows
• work with dry cattle
• work with rough cattle (drovers and dealers' dogs)
• work loading and penning sheep
• work in yards (shearers', dealers' and contractors' dogs)

No single dog is capable of this variety of performance. Training and environment therefore further divide the Border Collie into categories of hill dog, lowland sheepdog, cow dog, cattle dog, rough cattle dog and sheep dealer's dog.

nate and assert mastery over sheep without aggressive barking or biting. A dog with power holds authority over his flock without terrifying or spooking the sheep.

INTELLIGENCE

Intelligence in the Border Collie cannot be likened to that of his human master. It is so closely bound with working instinct and the desire to please that it may not be describable out of this context. In the working dog, intelligence is not inventive but innately correct when confronted with any decision involving the task for which it is bred. It is wonderfully clear but humanly puzzling in its adherence to a functional and practical hierarchy. Consider the dog's allegiance to her master, so unyielding that a bitch will allow that person to take her puppies away, without anger or objection.

TEMPERAMENT

The strongest desire bred into the Border Collie is the desire to work. This is the result of centuries of development and dominates even the survival instinct in some Collies. These dogs can become frustrated and destructive if they find themselves in an environment with nothing for them to do. A dog of this sort does not always make a good pet, and yet the careful and consider-

ate owner can surmount this instinctual difficulty by making his Border Collie a functional and important part of the family. Guarding his human family and their property is also demanding work. The important thing is to keep your dog interested, occupied and active. The ranch or farm, after all, has probably more down time built into its schedule than the average on-the-go, weather-impervious modern suburban family.

Dedication to work, which is obviously not a fault in the working dog, can result in neurotic pet dogs and is the consequence of breeding for performance rather than temperament. Nervousness, in general, is the most common personality problem in the Border Collie. There is, of course, only a fine line between the sensitively tuned working animal and one that exhibits nervousness. The distinction is related to environment and occupation.

The fact that obedience is such a strong instinct makes training the Border Collie a truly rewarding enterprise. No dog learns faster and retains what he has learned longer. Remember, however, that because your Border Collie is so eager to perform and please, and consequently so disappointed at failure, your training should be gentle while being firm. Rough bullying methods may seem to get obedience, but

WHAT'S IN A NAME?
There is more that goes into naming a Border Collie than meets the eye. While for a pet dog any name that you fancy is fine, there is a convention in the naming of working dogs. A working dog requires a short name that is simple to pronounce and will be unmistakably heard in the long-range, abrupt and often complicated communications of the farmer or shepherd. Classic popular names for males have been Ben, Lad, Roy and Cap; favorites for bitches have included Nell, Meg and Jess.

obedience without trust will soon be forgotten.

Shyness and sulkiness are other faults of temperament sometimes found in the Border Collie that may interfere with training. Again these faults are related to the dog's deep desire to perform; these dogs cannot bear to fail or disappoint their masters. Training such dogs is difficult, since they will not stand any correction, even the gentlest reproof.

The Border Collie can sometimes be a one-person animal, so attuned to his master that others may fail to elicit his attention or obedience. Pet dogs should be socialized early and handled by all members of the family in order to avoid this condition.

It is especially worthwhile to note the importance of exercise as relates to your Border Collie's mental (and, of course, physical) well-being. Do not think that a couple of daily walks on a lead will provide your Border Collie with enough exercise. You must find a secure open area (such as your fenced-in yard) in which your dog can run free for a period of time. Anything short of this may produce a neurotic, unhappy animal. As for outside housing, do not be surprised if you find your pet more often on the roof of his dog house than inside it.

Boredom and frustrated herding instincts may cause your dog to engage in a very dangerous behavior that, unfortunately, is rather common in pet Border Collies: car chasing. The combination of the instinctive "eye" and "outrun" with the lure of cars and local traffic is the leading cause of accidental death among pets of this breed. Sufficient activity and training will diminish this hazard but will never entirely eliminate it. Even when your Border Collie is completely trained, it is still necessary to keep him on lead in open areas and to let him off lead only in enclosed areas.

APPEARANCE
There are wide variations in the appearance of the Border Collie. This is the result of the attitude that the ability to work is far more important than the looks of the dog. The AKC breed standard

takes into account the practical nature of the animal and therefore allows exceptional variety in color, size and coat while demanding—above everything else—balance and soundness.

As long as appearance does not come to dominate the breeding and perception of the dog, there is certainly room in our admiration for the Border Collie to discuss, and even to idealize, some aspects of appearance.

The head shape should reveal at a glance the sex of the Collie. The classic type is wedge shaped, but smaller foxy types are often seen, as are pointer types with

A NOTE ABOUT HEALTH

The most serious hereditary defect in the Border Collie is progressive retinal atrophy (PRA), also known as "night blindness." Because this disease is controlled by a recessive gene, it is hard to eradicate in the breed. Its diagnosis is often uncertain because of its progressive nature. Some dogs never go completely blind, while others are blind by three or four years of age. Collie eye anomaly (CEA), a blinding condition prevalent in the Rough Collie, is relatively uncommon in the Border Collie.

Hip dysplasia is seen in the Border Collie, although it is not often readily evident in non-working dogs. Responsible breeders register their dogs' x-rays with the Orthopedic Foundation for Animals (OFA).

domed skulls. The ears may stand up, bend over or lie flat. Eyes should generally be brown, although blue eyes are quite common.

Conformation is extremely important because of its link to performance. The dog works with its head low, and a long neck is necessary for balance. Shoulders should be well laid back to facilitate speed and reduce jarring on sudden stops. Long legs and a broad chest mean more speed and plenty of lung and heart room. Length in the back and hips is necessary for stamina and grace. The tail should be carried low.

ously these dogs are not adequately protected from the demands of rough working conditions.

Many of the Border Collies registered today are black-and-white in color. The distribution of color can follow any pattern, but black dominance is preferred. Tri-colors (black, white and tan) are common. Variations of brown coloring, from russet to liver, are seen, as are grays and blue and red merles. While all colors and patterns are accepted, white markings have a utilitarian value because they help the farmer locate the dog in the field.

NATURAL APTITUDES AND ACTIVITIES

The Border Collie's instinctual abilities have been adapted to many activities other than herding and farming. One very well-known activity is the herding trial. While not exclusively a showcase for Border Collies, trials seem to be dominated by the breed. Sheepdog trials, the predecessor of today's herding trials, first began in 1873 as a way, when all is considered, to show off the hard-earned skills of a farmer's dog and to prove one's dog better than another's. Today the aim promoted by the International Sheep Dog Society is to improve the breed of sheepdogs for herding by encouraging competition. Sheepdog trials are based on farm

The breed is seen in two distinct coat types, smooth and rough; the preference for coat type is also dictated by practicality. Dogs with overly long coats are at a disadvantage in the field and in bad weather. Thorns, burs, mud and snow will collect on his belly and legs and between his pads. Such coats will invite fleas, encourage skin problems and engender a terrible smell when wet. Straight, silky hair with a dense undercoat is ideal. The smooth-coated dog is best in the practical sense. Border Collies can also be found with coats as fine as those of Greyhounds, but obvi-

Border Collies work hard, but they also need to rest in order to conserve their energies for work.

work or, more correctly, on the type of work done by a sheepdog on a hilly farm. They basically test the skills of outrun, lift, drive, pen and shed. The handler sends his dog from 200 to 400 yards to fetch a small number of sheep, usually four or five. The dog must run well out in order not to send the sheep back into the pens. The dog must then bring the sheep through a gate, steer them around the handler, drive them away and through another gate, turn them and drive them across the course, negotiate a third set of gates and then drive the sheep back to a gated pen. After this, the dog must send the sheep out of the pen and drive them off the course.

Obedience and agility are also two areas in which the Border Collie excels. Competition of both types are dominated by the breed. These trials celebrate the instinctive obedience and natural agility of the Border Collie. If you have ever observed one of these trials, you cannot help but notice that Border Collies are present in droves...and they consistently finish well. The relationship of these tests to the actual work for which the Border Collie was intended is marginal, but they offer a welcome outlet for the pet

Training a Border Collie can be quite a rewarding endeavor. Intelligence, trainability and willingness to please make the Border Collie very popular as a pet and companion.

dog's energy as well as training goals for dog and owner.

Border Collies are sometimes used as guide dogs for the blind, but more often the dogs used for this job are crossbred with either Labrador or Golden Retrievers. Pure-bred Border Collies are generally too quick and sudden in their movements for this occupation. Their hardiness and persistence, however, make them excellent choices for search and rescue animals. Bitches with short coats that resist snow and mud are preferred here. Borders used for this purpose should be relatively friendly and loose-eyed; that is, with less of the instinctual tendency to stop and level the mesmerizing stare known as "eye."

GOOD OWNER, GOOD PET

As often stated, the Border Collie is primarily a working dog, but this is not exclusively so. Its intelligence lends it a quality of adaptability that, given the right owner, may make pet life nearly as satisfying for the dog as the working career for which it was born and bred. So in the end we come back to our beginning consideration—human nature. Can the pet owner understand the needs of his Border Collie and mediate between the animal's instincts and its environment? If so, then this expertly engineered working dog can become an enjoyable pet. As with any breed, all other considerations aside, it is good owners who make good pets.

The face-off. Border Collies are experts at mesmerizing other animals with their stares.

BORDER COLLIE

While not the "main stage" of the Border Collie's auspicious talents, dog shows are another arena in which the breed's qualities are displayed. The conformation show is considered by some breed experts to present a danger to the carefully bred instincts of the Border Collie. The enthusiasm for dog shows has caused other working breeds to become mere caricatures of their former utilitarian selves.

A breed standard, which is a written description of an ideal representative of a breed, is used by judges and breeders to determine the relative merits and faults of a dog. By definition, such a standard must describe each part of the dog, keeping in mind the working attributes that make each physical attribute advantageous to the dog. The American Kennel Club breed standard for the Border Collie sets out to keep the

Profile of a mature dog, well balanced and structurally sound.

The Border Collie's expression, the general appearance of the head's features, should be alert and full of interest.

breed's working characteristics in view. Whether this attitude will remain and prevail is the responsibility of every true lover of the breed. While the Border Collie varies significantly in many working lines, where conformation is far less important than performance, breeders still attempt to balance the equation by producing handsome, harmonious dogs with outstanding working ability.

THE AMERICAN KENNEL CLUB STANDARD FOR THE BORDER COLLIE

Preamble—The Border Collie originated in the border country between Scotland and England where the shepherds' breeding selection was based on biddable stock sense and the ability to work long days on rugged terrain. As a result of this selective breeding, the Border Collie developed the unique working style of gathering and fetching the stock with wide sweeping outruns. The stock is then controlled with an intense gaze known as "eye," coupled with a stalking style of movement. This selective breeding over hundreds of years developed the Border Collie's intensity, energy and trainability which are features so important that they are equal to physical size and appearance. The Border Collie has extraordinary instinct and an uncanny ability to reason. One of its greatest assets is the ability to work out of sight of its master without commands. Breeding based on this working ability has made this breed the world's premier sheep herding dog, a job the Border Collie is still used for worldwide.

General Appearance

The Border Collie is a well balanced, medium-sized dog of athletic appearance, displaying style and agility in equal measure with soundness and strength. Its hard, muscular body conveys the impression of effortless movement and endless endurance. The Border Collie is extremely intelligent, with its keen, alert expression being a very important characteristic of the breed. Any aspect of structure or temperament that would impede the dog's ability to function as a herding dog should be severely faulted. The Border Collie is, and should remain, a natural and unspoiled true working sheep dog whose conformation is described herein. Honorable scars and broken teeth incurred in the line of duty are acceptable.

Size, Proportion, Substance

The height at the withers varies from 19 to 22 inches for males, 18 to 21 inches for females. The body, from prosternum to point of buttocks, is slightly longer than the height at the withers with the length to height ratio being approximately 10:9. Bone must be strong, medium being correct but lighter bone is preferred over heavy. Overall balance between height, length, weight and bone is crucial and is more important than any absolute measurement. Dogs must be presented in hard working condition. Excess body weight is not to be mistaken for muscle or substance. Any single feature of size appearing out of proportion should be considered a fault.

Head

Expression is intelligent, alert, eager, and full of interest. *Eyes* are set well apart, of moderate size, oval in shape. The color encompasses the full range of brown eyes; dogs having body colors other than black may have noticeably lighter eye color. Blue eyes

Head study of an adult dog of pleasing type, correct structure and proportion.

(with one, both or part of one or both eyes being blue) in dogs other than merle, are acceptable but not preferred. Eye rims should be fully pigmented, lack thereof considered a fault according to degree. *Ears* are of medium size, set well apart, one or both carried erect and/or semi-erect (varying from 1/4 to 3/4 of the ear erect). When semi-erect, the tips may fall forward or outward to the side. Ears are sensitive and mobile. *Skull* is relatively flat and moderate in width. The skull and muzzle are approximately equal in length. In profile the top of the skull is parallel with the top of the muzzle. *Stop* moderate, but distinct. The *muzzle* is strong, tapering slightly to the nose. The underjaw is strong and well

developed. A domed, blocky or very narrow skull is faulty according to degree, as is cheekiness and a snipey muzzle. *Nose* color matches the primary body color. Nostrils are well developed. Lack of nose pigmentation is a fault according to degree. *Bite*—Teeth and jaws are strong, meeting in a scissors bite. Complete dentition is required. Missing molars or premolars are serious faults as is an undershot or overshot bite.

Neck, Topline, Body
Neck is of proportional length to the body, strong and muscular, slightly arched and blending smoothly into the shoulders. *Topline*—Back is level from behind the withers to the slightly arched, muscular loins, falling to a gently sloping croup. *Body* is athletic in appearance with a deep, moderately broad chest reaching no further than the point of the elbow. The rib cage is moderately long with well sprung ribs. Loins moderately deep and short, muscular, slightly arched and with a slight but distinct tuck up. The tail is set on low and is moderately long with the bone reaching at least to the hock. The ideal tail carriage is low when the dog is concentrating on a given task and may have a slight upward swirl at the end like a shepherd's crook. In excitement, it may be raised proudly and waved like a banner, showing a confident personality. A tail curled over the back is a fault.

Forequarters
Forelegs should be parallel when viewed from front, pasterns

slightly sloping when viewed from side. Because sufficient length of leg is crucial for the type of work the breed is required to do, the distance from the withers to the elbow is slightly less than from the elbow to the ground and legs that are too short in proportion to the rest of the body are a serious fault. The shoulder blades are long, well laid back and well-angulated to the upper arm. Shoulder blades and upper arms are equal in length. There is sufficient width between the tops of the shoulder blades to allow for the characteristic crouch when approaching and moving stock. The elbows are neither in nor out. Feet are compact, oval in shape; pads deep and strong, toes moderately arched and close together with strong nails of moderate length. Dewclaws may be removed.

Hindquarters
Broad and muscular, in profile sloping gracefully to the low set tail. The thighs are long, broad, deep and muscular. Stifles are well turned with strong hocks that may be either parallel or very slightly turned in. Dewclaws should be removed. Feet, although slightly smaller, are the same as front.

Coat
Two varieties are permissible, both having close-fitting, dense,

weather resistant double coats with the top coat either straight or wavy and coarser in texture than the undercoat which is soft, short and dense. The rough variety is medium in length without being excessive. Forelegs, haunches, chest and underside are feathered and the coat on face, ears, feet, fronts of legs is short and smooth.

The Border Collie's coat, whether rough or smooth, should be dense and close-fitting.

The Border Collie should appear natural, without any trimming or sculpting.

The smooth variety is short over entire body, is usually coarser in texture than the rough variety and may have slight feathering on forelegs, haunches, chest and ruff. Neither coat type is preferred over the other. Seasonal shedding is

FAULTS IN PROFILE

Generally coarse head and body, lacking in flexibility; upright loaded shoulders; low on leg; poor topline and tail carriage; pigeon-toed in front, lacking sufficient rear angulation.

Structurally unsound body, lacking substance; upright shoulders; narrow front; toes out; long back and weak topline; high in rear; cow-hocked; kinked tail.

normal and should not be penalized. The Border Collie's purpose as an actively working herding dog shall be clearly evident in its presentation. Excess hair on the feet, hock and pastern areas may be neatened for the show ring. Whiskers are untrimmed. Dogs that are overly groomed (trimmed and/or sculpted) should be penalized according to the extent.

Color
The Border Collie appears in all colors or combination of colors and/or markings. Solid color, bi-color, tri-color, merle and sable dogs are to be judged equally with no one color or pattern preferred over another. White markings may

be clear white or ticked to any degree. Random white patches on the body and head are permissible but should not predominate. Color and markings are always secondary to physical evaluation and gait.

Gait

The Border Collie is an agile dog, able to suddenly change speed and direction while maintaining balance and grace. Endurance is its trademark. The Border Collie's most used working gaits are the gallop and a moving crouch (stealth) which convert to a balanced and free trot, with minimum lift of the feet. The head is carried level with or slightly below the withers. When shown, Border Collies should move on a loose lead and at moderate speed, never raced around the ring with the head held high. When viewed from the side the trot is not long striding, yet covers the ground with minimum effort, exhibiting facility of movement rather than a hard driving action. Exaggerated reach and drive at the trot are not useful to the Border Collie. The topline is firm. Viewed from the front, action is forward and true without wasted motion. Viewed from the rear, hindquarters drive with thrust and flexibility with hocks turning neither in nor out, moving close together but never touching. The legs, both front and rear, tend to converge toward the

center line as speed increases. Any deficiency that detracts from efficient movement is a fault.

Attractive in any color, the Border Collie is usually seen with white markings, though these are not required.

Temperament

The Border Collie is energetic, intelligent, keen, alert, and responsive. An intense worker of great tractability, it is affectionate towards friends but may be sensibly reserved towards strangers. When approached, the Border Collie should stand its ground. It should be alert and interested, never showing fear, dullness or resentment. Any tendencies toward viciousness, nervousness or shyness are very serious faults.

Faults

Any deviation from the foregoing should be considered a fault, the seriousness of the fault depending upon the extent of the deviation.

Approved January 13, 2004
Effective March 2, 2004

BORDER COLLIE

FINDING AND SELECTING A BORDER COLLIE PUPPY

If you are convinced that the Border Collie is the ideal dog for you, it's time to learn about where to find a puppy and what to look for. Locating a litter of Border Collies should not present a problem for the new owner. You should inquire about breeders in your area who enjoy a good reputation in the breed. You are looking for an established breeder with outstanding dog ethics and a strong commitment to the breed. New owners should have as many questions as they have doubts. An established breeder is indeed the one to answer your four million questions and make you comfortable with your choice of the Border Collie. An established breeder will sell you a puppy at a fair price if, and only if, the breeder determines that you are a suitable, worthy owner of his dogs. An established breeder can be relied upon for advice with regard to feeding, training, health and more. A reputable breeder will accept a puppy back, without questions, should you decide that this is not the right dog for you.

When choosing a breeder, reputation is much more important than convenience of location. Do not be impressed by breeders who run brag advertisements in the magazines about their stupendous champions and working lines. Many quality breeders are quiet and unassuming. You hear about them at the dog trials and shows, by word of mouth. You may be well advised to avoid the novice who lives only a couple miles away. A backyard breeder, trying so hard to get rid of that first litter of puppies, is more than accommodating and anxious to

THE FAMILY TREE

Your puppy's pedigree is his family tree. Just as a child may resemble his parents and grandparents, so too will a puppy reflect the qualities, good and bad, of his ancestors, especially those in the first two generations. Therefore it's important to know as much as possible about a puppy's immediate relatives. Reputable and experienced breeders should be able to explain the pedigree and why they chose to breed from the particular dogs they used.

sell you one. That breeder will charge you as much as any established breeder. Also he isn't going to interrogate you and your family about your intentions with the puppy, the environment and training you can provide, etc. That breeder will be nowhere to be found when your poorly bred, badly adjusted four-pawed monster starts to growl and spit up at midnight or eat the family cat!

While health considerations in the Border Collie are not nearly as daunting as in most other breeds, socialization is a breeder concern of immense importance. Since the Border Collie's temperament can vary from line to line, socialization is the first and best way to encourage a proper, stable personality.

Choosing a breeder is an important first step in dog ownership. Fortunately, the majority of Border Collie breeders are devoted to the breed and its well-being. New owners should have little problem finding a reputable breeder who doesn't live in a different state. The American Kennel Club and any of the Border Collie registries or clubs are able to recommend breeders of quality Border Collies. Potential owners are encouraged to attend herding trials and tests as well as dog shows to see the Border Collies in action, to meet the handlers firsthand and find out

about the breed's requirements and characteristics. Provided you approach the handlers when they are not too busy with the dogs, most are more than willing to answer questions, recommend breeders and give advice. By observing Border Collies at shows and trials, you will get an idea about the style and type of dog that appeals to you—the plush-coated show dog, the sleek working dog, the smooth-coated dog and so on.

Now that you have contacted and met a breeder or two and made your choice about which breeder is best suited to your needs, it's time to visit the litter. Keep in mind that most good breeders have waiting lists. Sometimes new owners have to wait as long as two years for a puppy. If you are really commit-

MEET THE PARENTS

Because puppies are a combination of genes inherited from both of their parents, they will reflect the qualities and temperament of their sire and dam. When visiting a litter of pups, spend time with the dam and observe her behavior with her puppies, the breeder and with strangers. The sire is often not on the premises, but the dam should be with her pups until they are seven or eight weeks old. If either parent is surly, quarrelsome or fearful, it's likely that some of the pups will inherit those tendencies.

Your breeder can help evaluate your Border Collie pup's conformation if you plan to show your dog.

are many more considerations. The parents of a future working dog should have excellent qualifications, including actual work experience as well as working titles in their pedigrees. The AKC awards herding titles to outstanding working dogs, as do some other clubs. You may see AKC herding test titles like HT and PT or better yet herding trial titles like HX and HCh. Do not rely solely on AKC titles in the pedigree, however; the breeders should have a commercial livestock operation and have dogs that have won in sanctioned sheepdog or cattledog trials.

ted to the breeder whom you've selected, then you will wait (and hope for an early arrival). If not, you may have to resort to your second-or third- choice breeder.

If you are choosing a Border Collie as a pet dog and not a working dog, you simply should select a pup that is friendly and attractive. Border Collies generally have small litters, averaging five puppies, so selection is limited once you have located a desirable litter. While the basic structure of the breed has little variation, the temperament may present trouble in certain strains. Beware of the shy or overly aggressive puppy: be especially conscious of the nervous Border Collie pup. Do not let sentiment or emotion trap you into buying the runt of the litter.

If you intend to have your new charge herding sheep, there

The sex of your puppy is largely a matter of personal taste, although there is a common belief among those who work with Border Collies that bitches are quicker to learn and generally more loving and faithful. Males learn

MALE OR FEMALE?

Males of most dog breeds tend to be larger than their female counterparts and take longer to mature. Males also can be more dominant and territorial, especially if they are intact. Neutering before one year of age can help minimize those tendencies. Females of most breeds are often less rambunctious and easier to handle. However, individual personalities vary, so the differences are often due more to temperament than to the sex of the animal.

SELECTING FROM THE LITTER

Before you visit a litter of puppies, promise yourself that you won't fall for the first pretty face you see! Decide on your goals for your puppy—herding dog, show prospect, obedience competitor, family companion—and then look for a puppy who displays the appropriate qualities. In most litters, there is an Alpha pup (the bossy puppy), and occasionally a shy fellow who is less confident, with the rest of the litter falling somewhere in the middle. "Middle-of-the-roaders" are safe bets for most families and novice competitors.

more slowly but retain their lessons longer. The difference in size is noticeable but slight. Coloration should not be a grave concern with this breed, although there have been countless treatises upon the desirable amount of white and black on sheepdogs. There's the ever-popular "black-sheep" theory that claims that too much black on a Collie will frighten the sheep, which only accept white animals in their flocks. This might seem like good sense or nonsense, depending on your family's feelings about its black sheep! Nevertheless, a good stable dog, with working abilities, can be any color and owners should curb their preconceived notions about the color of their Collies.

Because litters are small and because Border Collies are primarily workers rather than pets, commercial breeders are less attracted to the breed. This also helps your selection, ensuring that most pups will come from strong working lines unencumbered by poor breeding practices. The cost for a puppy in a rural area will generally be lower than that of other breeds but higher in city areas where a percentage of the dogs will be sold for pets or show dogs. Look in farming/ranching newspapers and journals like *Stockdog Magazine, National Stockdog Magazine, American Border Collie Magazine* and *The Working Border Collie* to find the best working Border Collies.

Breeders commonly allow visitors to see the litter by around the fifth or sixth week, and puppies leave for their new homes between the eighth and tenth week. Some breeders may keep a puppy or two for a few months to see if they turn out to be potential show dogs. Often these pups make excellent choices.

Young puppies need to learn the rules of the trade from their dam, and most dams continue teaching the pups manners and dos and don'ts until around the eighth week. Breeders spend significant amounts of time with the Border Collie toddlers so that they are able to interact with the "other species," i.e., humans.

Puppy teeth can be misleading... although small, they are very sharp and capable of inflicting pain.

Given the long history that dogs and humans have, bonding between the two species is natural but must be nurtured. A well-bred, well-socialized Border Collie pup wants nothing more than to be near you and please you.

Always check the bite of your selected puppy to be sure that it is

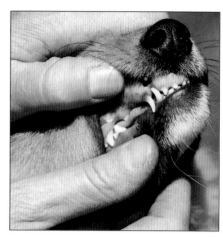

As a young Border Collie loses his puppy teeth, they are replaced with strong adult teeth. This Border Collie has a clean, healthy smile.

PEDIGREE VS. REGISTRATION CERTIFICATE

Too often new owners are confused between these two important documents. Your puppy's pedigree, essentially a family tree, is a written record of a dog's genealogy of three generations or more. The pedigree will show you the names as well as performance titles of all dogs in your pup's background. Your breeder must provide you with a registration application, with his part properly filled out. You must complete the application and send it to the AKC with the proper fee. Every puppy must come from a litter that has been AKC-registered by the breeder, born in the US and from a sire and dam that are also registered with the AKC.

The seller must provide you with complete records to identify the puppy. The AKC requires that the seller provide the buyer with the following: breed; sex, color and markings; date of birth; litter number (when available); names and registration numbers of the parents; breeder's name; and date sold or delivered.

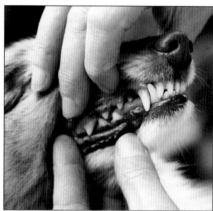

neither overshot nor undershot. This may not be too noticeable on a young puppy but it is a fairly common problem with certain lines of Border Collies.

A COMMITTED NEW OWNER

By now you should understand what makes the Border Collie a most unique and special dog, one that may fit nicely into your family and lifestyle. If you have researched breeders, you should be able to recognize a knowledge-able and responsible Border Collie breeder who cares not only about his pups but also about what kind of owner you will be. If you have completed the final step in your new journey, you have found a litter, or possibly two, of quality Border Collie pups.

A visit with the puppies and their breeder should be an education in itself. Breed research, breeder selection and puppy visitation are very important aspects of finding the puppy of your dreams. Beyond that, these things also lay the foundation for a successful future with your pup. Puppy personalities within each litter vary, from the shy and easygoing puppy to the one who is dominant and assertive, with most pups falling somewhere in between. By spending time with the puppies you will be able to recognize certain behaviors and what these behaviors indicate about each pup's temperament. Which type of pup will complement your family dynamic is best determined by observing the puppies in action within their "pack."

Your breeder's expertise and recommendations are also valuable. Although you may fall in love with a bold and brassy male, the breeder may suggest that another pup would be best for you. The breeder's experience in rearing Border Collie pups and matching their temperaments with appropri-

Border Collies become completely dedicated to their owners. Be sure you are ready to reciprocate this love and devotion, as your pet Border Collie depends on you for proper care.

ate humans offers the best assurance that your pup will meet your needs and expectations. The type of puppy that you select is just as important as your decision that the Border Collie is the breed for you.

The decision to live with a Border Collie is a serious commitment and not one to be taken lightly. This puppy is a living sentient being that will be dependent on you for basic survival for his entire life. Beyond the basics of survival—food, water, shelter and protection—he needs much, much more. The new pup needs love, nurturing and a good canine education to mold him into a responsible, well-behaved canine citizen.

Your Border Collie's health and good manners will need consistent monitoring and regular "tune-ups," so your job as a responsible dog owner will be ongoing throughout every stage of his life. If you are not prepared to accept these responsibilities and commit to them for the next decade, likely longer, then you are not prepared to own a dog of any breed.

Although the responsibilities of owning a dog may at times tax your patience, the joy of living with a Border Collie far outweighs the workload. The author assures you that a well-mannered adult dog will be worth your time and effort. Before your very eyes, your new charge will grow up to be your most loyal friend, devoted to you unconditionally.

YOUR BORDER COLLIE SHOPPING LIST

Just as expectant parents prepare a nursery for their baby, so should you ready your home for the arrival of your Border Collie pup. If you have the necessary puppy supplies purchased and in place before he comes home, it will ease the puppy's transition from the warmth and familiarity of his mom and littermates to the brand-new environment of his new home and human family. You will be too busy to stock up and prepare your house after your pup comes home, that's for sure! Imagine how a pup must feel upon being transported to a strange new place. It's up to you to comfort him and to let your little pup know that he is going to be happy with you.

FOOD AND WATER BOWLS

Your puppy will need separate bowls for his food and water.

A pair of sturdy ceramic bowls, not too heavy but durable, is an attractive option for indoor feeding.

Stainless steel pans are generally preferred over plastic bowls since they sterilize better and pups are less inclined to chew on the metal. Heavy-duty ceramic bowls are popular, but consider how often you will have to pick up those heavy bowls. Buy adult-sized pans, as your puppy will grow into them before you know it.

THE DOG CRATE

If you think that crates are tools of punishment and confinement for when a dog has misbehaved, think again. Most breeders and almost all trainers recommend a crate as the preferred house-training aid as well as for all-around puppy training and safety. Because dogs are natural den creatures that prefer cave-like environments, the benefits of crate use are many. The crate provides the puppy with his very own "safe house," a cozy place to sleep, take a break or seek comfort with a favorite toy; a travel aid to house your dog when on the road, at motels or at the vet's office; a training aid to help teach your puppy proper toileting habits; a place of solitude when non-dog people happen to drop by and don't want a lively puppy—or even a well-behaved adult dog—saying hello or begging for attention.

Crates come in several types, although the wire crate and the fiberglass airline-type crate are the most popular. Both are safe and

CRATE EXPECTATIONS

To make the crate more inviting to your puppy, you can offer his first meal or two inside the crate, always keeping the crate door open so that he does not feel confined. Keep a favorite toy or two in the crate for him to play with while inside. You can also cover the crate at night with a lightweight sheet to make it more den-like and remove the stimuli of household activity. Never put him into his crate as punishment or as you are scolding him, since he will then associate his crate with negative situations and avoid going there.

your puppy will adjust to either one, so the choice is up to you. The wire crates offer better visibility for the pup as well as better ventilation. Many of the wire crates easily collapse into suitcase-size carriers. The fiberglass crates, similar to those used by

Border Collies on their way to a dog show. Whether you own one Border Collie or a truckload, dogs should always be secure in their crates when traveling.

the airlines for animal transport, are sturdier and more den-like. However, the fiberglass crates do not collapse and are less ventilated than a wire crate, which can be problematic in hot weather. Some of the newer crates are made of heavy plastic mesh; they are very lightweight and fold up into slim-line suitcases. However, a mesh crate might not be suitable for a pup with manic chewing habits.

Don't bother with a puppy-sized crate. Although your Border Collie will be a wee fellow when you bring him home, he will grow up in the blink of an eye and your puppy crate will be useless. Purchase a crate that will accommodate an adult Border Collie. He will stand about 21-22 inches when full grown, so a medium- to large-sized crate will fit him nicely.

BEDDING AND CRATE PADS

Your puppy will enjoy some type of soft bedding in his "room" (the crate), something he can snuggle into to feel cozy and secure. Old towels or blankets are good choices for a young pup, since he may (and probably will) have a toileting accident or two in the crate or decide to chew on the bedding material. Once he is fully trained and out of the early chewing stage, you can replace the puppy bedding with a permanent crate pad if you prefer. Crate pads and other dog beds run the gamut from inexpensive to high-end doggie-designer styles, but don't splurge on the good stuff until you are sure that your puppy is reliable and won't tear it up or make a mess on it.

ROCK-A-BYE BEDDING

The wide assortment of dog beds today can make your choice quite difficult, as there are many adorable novelty beds in fun styles and prints. It's wise to wait until your puppy has outgrown the chewing stage before providing him with a dog bed, since he might make confetti out of it. Your puppy will be happy with an old towel or blanket in his crate until he is old enough to resist the temptation to chew up his bed. For a dog of any age, a bed with a washable cover is always a wise choice.

PUPPY TOYS

Just as infants and older children require objects to stimulate their minds and bodies, puppies need toys to entertain their curious brains, wiggly paws and achy teeth. A fun array of safe doggie toys will help satisfy your puppy's chewing instincts and distract him from gnawing on the leg of your antique chair or your new leather sofa. Most puppy toys are cute and look as if they would be a lot of fun, but not all are necessarily safe or good for your puppy, so use caution when you go puppy-toy shopping.

Although Border Collies are not known to be voracious chewers like many other dogs, they still love to chew. The best "chewcifiers" are nylon and hard rubber bones which are safe to gnaw on and come in sizes appropriate for the Border Collie. Be especially careful of natural bones, which can splinter or develop dangerous sharp edges; pups can easily swallow or choke on those bone splinters. Veterinarians often tell of surgical nightmares involving bits of splintered bone, because in addition to the danger of choking, the sharp pieces can damage the intestinal tract.

Similarly, rawhide chews, while a favorite of most dogs and puppies, can be equally dangerous. Pieces of rawhide are easily swallowed after they get all gummy from chewing, and dogs have been known to choke on large pieces of ingested rawhide. Rawhide chews should be offered only when you can supervise the puppy.

TOYS 'R SAFE

The vast array of tantalizing puppy is staggering. Stroll through any pet shop or pet-supply outlet and you will see that the choices can be overwhelming. However, not all dog toys are safe or sensible. Most very young puppies enjoy soft woolly toys that they can snuggle with and carry around. (You know they have outgrown them when they shred them up!) Avoid toys that have buttons, tabs or other enhancements that can be chewed off and swallowed. Soft toys that squeak are fun, but make sure your puppy does not disembowel the toy and remove (and swallow) the squeaker. Toys that rattle or make noise can excite a puppy, but they present the same danger as the squeaky kind and so require supervision. Hard rubber toys that bounce can also entertain a pup, but make sure that the toy is too big for your pup to swallow

Soft woolly toys are special puppy favorites. They come in a wide variety of cute shapes and sizes; some look like little stuffed animals. Puppies love to shake them up and toss them about, or simply carry them around. Be careful of fuzzy toys that have button eyes or noses that your pup could chew off and swallow, and make sure that he does not disembowel a squeaky toy to remove the squeaker! Braided rope toys are similar in that they are fun to chew and toss around, but they shred easily and the strings are easy to swallow. The strings are not digestible and, if the puppy doesn't pass them in his stool, he could end up at the vet's office. As with rawhides, your puppy should be closely monitored with rope toys.

If you believe that your pup has ingested one of these forbidden objects, check his stools for the next couple of days to see if he passes them when he defecates. At the same time, also watch for signs of intestinal distress. A call to your veterinarian might be in order to get his advice and be on the safe side.

An all-time favorite toy for puppies (young and old!) is the empty gallon milk jug. Hard plastic juice containers—46 ounces or more—are also excellent. Such containers make lots of noise when they are batted about, and puppies go crazy with delight as they play with them. However,

Puppies love soft fuzzy toys to carry around. Always monitor your Border Collie when he's playing with rope toys.

COLLARING OUR CANINES

The standard flat collar with a buckle or a snap, in leather, nylon or cotton, is widely regarded as the everyday all-purpose collar. If the collar fits correctly, you should be able to fit two fingers between the collar and the dog's neck.

Leather Buckle Collars

The martingale, Greyhound or limited-slip collar is preferred by many dog owners and trainers. It is fixed with an extra loop that tightens when pressure is applied to the leash. The martingale collar gets tighter but does not "choke" the dog. The limited-slip collar should only be used for walking and training, not for free play or interaction with another dog. These types of collar should never be left on the dog, as the extra loop can lead to accidents.

Limited-Slip Collar

Choke collars, usually made of stainless steel, are made for training purposes, though are not recommended for small dogs or heavily coated breeds. The chains can injure small dogs or damage long/abundant coats. Thin nylon choke leads are commonly used on show dogs while in the ring, though they are not practical for everyday use.

The harness, with two or three straps that attach over the dog's shoulders and around his torso, is a humane and safe alternative to the conventional collar. By and large, a well-made harness is virtually escape-proof. Harnesses are available in nylon and mesh and can be outfitted on most dogs, ranging in chest girths of from 10 to 30 inches.

Snap Bolt Choke Collar

Harness

Nylon Collar

Quick-Click Closure

Snake Chain

Chrome Steel

Fur-Saver

Choke Chain Collars

A head collar, composed of a nylon strap that goes around the dog's muzzle and a second strap that wraps around his neck, offers the owner better control over his dog. This device is recommended for problem-solving with dogs (including jumping up, pulling and aggressive behaviors), but must be used with care.

A training halter, including a flat collar and two straps, made of nylon and webbing, is designed for walking. There are several on the market; some are more difficult to put on the dog than others. The halter harness, with two small slip rings at each end, is recommended for ease of use.

LEASH LIFE

Dogs love leashes! Believe it or not, most dogs dance for joy every time their owners pick up their leashes. The leash means that the dog is going for a walk—and there are few things more exciting than that! Here are some of the kinds of leashes that are commercially available.

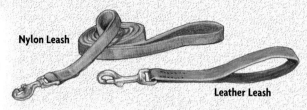

Nylon Leash

Leather Leash

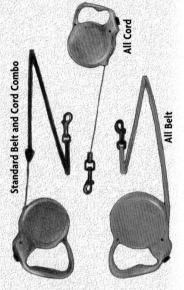

Standard Belt and Cord Combo

All Cord

All Belt

Retractable Leashes

Traditional Leash: Made of cotton, nylon or leather, these leashes are usually about 6 feet in length. A quality-made leather leash is softer on the hands than a nylon one. Durable woven cotton is a popular option. Lengths can vary up to about 48 feet, designed for different uses.

Chain Leash: Usually a metal chain leash with a plastic handle. This is not the best choice for most breeds, as it is heavier than other leashes and difficult to manage.

Retractable Leash: A long nylon cord is housed in a plastic device for extending and retracting. This leash, is ideal for taking trained dogs for long walks in open areas, although it is not recommended for large, powerful breeds. Different lengths and sizes are available, so check that you purchase one appropriate for your dog's weight.

Elastic Leash: A nylon leash with an elastic extension. This is useful for well-trained dogs, especially in conjunction with a head halter.

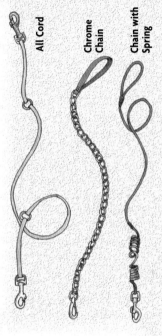

All Cord

Chrome Chain

Chain with Spring

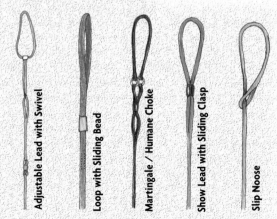

Adjustable Lead with Swivel

Loop with Sliding Bead

Martingale / Humane Choke

Show Lead with Sliding Clasp

Slip Noose

A Variety of Collar-Leash-in-One Products

Avoid leashes that are completely elastic, as they afford minimal control to the handler.

Adjustable Leash: This has two snaps, one on each end, and several metal rings. It is handy if you need to tether your dog temporarily, but is never to be used with a choke collar.

Tab Leash: A short leash (4 to 6 inches long) that attaches to your dog's collar. This device serves like a handle, in case you have to grab your dog while he's exercising off lead. It's ideal for "half-trained" dogs or dogs that listen only half the time.

Slip Leash: Essentially a leash with a collar built in, similar to what a dog-show handler uses to show a dog. This British-style collar has a ring on the end so that you can form a slip collar. Useful if you have to catch your own runaway dog or a stray.

they don't often last very long, so be sure to remove and replace them when they get chewed up on the ends.

A word of caution about home-made toys: be careful with your choices of non-traditional play objects. Never use old shoes or socks, since a puppy cannot distinguish between the old ones on which he's allowed to chew and the new ones in your closet that are strictly off limits. That principle applies to anything that resembles something that you don't want your puppy to chew up.

COLLARS

A lightweight nylon collar is the best choice for a very young pup. Quick-clip collars are easy to put on and remove, and they can be adjusted as the puppy grows. Introduce him to his collar as soon as he comes home to get him accustomed to wearing it. He'll get used to it quickly and won't mind a bit. Make sure that it is snug enough that it won't slip off, yet loose enough to be comfortable for the pup. You should be able to slip two fingers between the collar and his neck. Check the collar often, as puppies grow in spurts, and his collar can become too tight almost overnight. Choke collars are for training purposes only and should never be used on a puppy under four or five months old. Avoid using the chain chokers, as these can damage the Border Collie's coat.

LEASHES

A 6-foot nylon lead is an excellent choice for a young puppy. It is lightweight and not as tempting to chew as a leather lead. You can switch to a 6-foot leather lead after your pup has grown and is used to walking politely on a lead. For initial puppy walks and house-training purposes, you should invest in a shorter lead so that you have more control over the puppy. At first, you don't want him

Don't switch to a retractable lead until your Border Collie puppy has become heel trained.

wandering too far away from you, and when taking him out for toileting you will want to keep him in the specific area chosen for his potty spot.

Once the puppy is heel trained with a traditional leash, you can consider purchasing a retractable lead. A retractable lead is excellent for walking adult dogs that are already leash-wise. This lead allows the dog to roam farther away from you and explore a wider area when out walking, and also retracts when you need to keep him close to you.

HOME SAFETY FOR YOUR PUPPY

The importance of puppy-proofing cannot be overstated. In addition to making your house comfortable for your Border Collie's arrival, you also must make sure that your house is safe for your puppy before you bring him home. There are countless hazards in the owner's personal living environment that a pup can sniff, chew, swallow or destroy. Many are obvious; others are not. Do a thorough advance house check to remove or rearrange those things that could hurt your puppy,

Border Collie pups love to run and explore. Ensure your pup's safety in open areas by keeping him on a lead.

A Dog-Safe Home

The dog-safety police are taking you and your new puppy on a house tour. Let's go room by room and see how safe your own home is for your new pup. The following items are doggie dangers, so either they must be removed or the dog should be monitored or not have access to these areas.

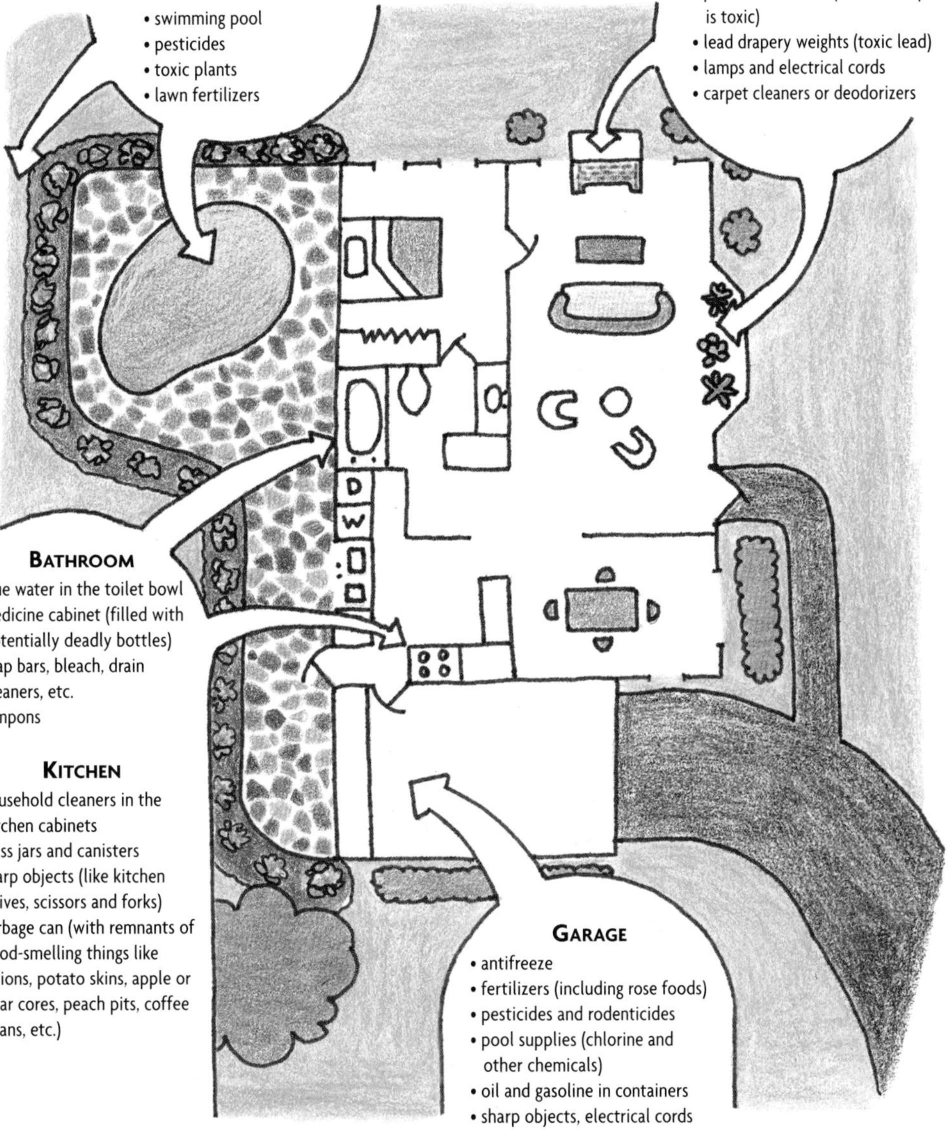

Living Room

- house plants (some varieties are poisonous)
- fireplace or wood-burning stove
- paint on the walls (lead-based paint is toxic)
- lead drapery weights (toxic lead)
- lamps and electrical cords
- carpet cleaners or deodorizers

Outdoor

- swimming pool
- pesticides
- toxic plants
- lawn fertilizers

Bathroom

- blue water in the toilet bowl
- medicine cabinet (filled with potentially deadly bottles)
- soap bars, bleach, drain cleaners, etc.
- tampons

Kitchen

- household cleaners in the kitchen cabinets
- glass jars and canisters
- sharp objects (like kitchen knives, scissors and forks)
- garbage can (with remnants of good-smelling things like onions, potato skins, apple or pear cores, peach pits, coffee beans, etc.)

Garage

- antifreeze
- fertilizers (including rose foods)
- pesticides and rodenticides
- pool supplies (chlorine and other chemicals)
- oil and gasoline in containers
- sharp objects, electrical cords and power tools

keeping any potentially dangerous items out of areas to which he will have access.

Electrical cords are especially dangerous, since puppies view them as irresistible chew toys. Unplug and remove all exposed cords or fasten them beneath a baseboard where the puppy cannot reach them. Veterinarians and firefighters can tell you horror stories about electrical burns and house fires that resulted from puppy-chewed electrical cords. Consider this a most serious precaution for your puppy and the rest of your family.

Scout your home for tiny objects that might be seen at a pup's eye level. Keep medication bottles and cleaning supplies well out of reach, and do the same with waste baskets and other trash containers. It goes without saying that you should not use rodent poison or other toxic chemicals in any puppy area and that you must keep such containers safely locked up. You will be amazed at how many places a curious puppy can discover!

Once your house has cleared inspection, check your yard. A sturdy fence, well embedded into the ground, will give your dog a safe place to play and potty. Although Border Collies are not known to be climbers or fence jumpers, they are still athletic dogs, so a 5- to 6-foot-high fence should be adequate to contain an agile youngster or adult. Check the fence periodically for necessary repairs. If there is a weak link or space to squeeze through, you can be sure a determined Border Collie will discover it.

The garage and shed can be hazardous places for a pup, as things like fertilizers, chemicals and tools are usually kept there. It's best to keep these areas off limits to the pup. Antifreeze is especially dangerous to dogs, as they find the taste appealing and it takes only a few licks from the driveway to kill a dog, puppy or adult, small breed or large.

VISITING THE VETERINARIAN

A good veterinarian is your Border Collie puppy's best health-insurance policy. If you do not already have a vet, ask friends and experienced dog people in your area for recommendations so that you can select a vet before you bring your Border Collie puppy home. Also arrange for your puppy's first veterinary examination beforehand, since many vets have two- and three-week waiting periods and your puppy should visit the vet within a day or so of coming home.

It's important to make sure your puppy's first visit to the vet

is a pleasant and positive one. The vet should take great care to befriend the pup and handle him gently to make their first meeting a positive experience. The vet will give the pup a thorough physical examination and set up a schedule for vaccinations and other necessary wellness visits. Be sure to show your vet any health and inoculation records, which you should have received from your breeder. Your vet is a great source of canine health information, so be sure to ask questions and take notes. Creating a health journal for your puppy will make a handy reference for his wellness and any future health problems that may arise.

Discuss an inoculation schedule with your vet. Your breeder should provide you with documents pertaining to which shots the pup has already received.

MEETING THE FAMILY

Your Border Collie's homecoming is an exciting time for all members of the family, and it's only natural that everyone will be

THE FAMILY FELINE

A resident cat has feline squatter's rights. The cat will treat the newcomer (your puppy) as she sees fit, regardless of what you do or say. So it's best to let the two of them work things out on their own terms. Cats have a height advantage and will generally leap to higher ground to avoid direct contact with a rambunctious pup. Some will hiss and boldly swat at a pup who passes by or tries to reach the cat. Keep the puppy under control in the presence of the cat and they will eventually become accustomed to each other.

Here's a hint: move the cat's litter box where the puppy can't get into it! It's best to do so well before the pup comes home so the cat is used to the new location.

HAPPY PUPPIES COME RUNNING

Never call your puppy (or adult dog) to come to you and then scold him or discipline him when he gets there. He will make a natural association between coming to you and being scolded, and he will think he was a bad dog for coming to you. He will then be reluctant to come whenever he is called. Always praise your puppy every time he comes to you.

eager to meet him, pet him and play with him. However, for the puppy's sake, it's best to make these initial family meetings as uneventful as possible so that the pup is not overwhelmed with too much too soon. Remember, he has just left his dam and his littermates and is away from the breeder's home for the first time. Despite his fuzzy wagging tail, he is still apprehensive and wondering where he is and who all these strange humans are. It's best to let him explore on his own and meet the family members as he feels comfortable. Let him investigate all the new smells, sights and sounds at his own pace. Children should be especially careful to not get overly excited, use loud voices or hug the pup too tightly. Be calm, gentle and affectionate, and be ready to comfort him if he appears frightened or uneasy.

Be sure to show your puppy his new crate during this first day home. Toss a treat or two inside the crate; if he associates the crate with food, he will associate the crate with good things. If he is comfortable with the crate, you can offer him his first meal inside it. Leave the door ajar so he can wander in and out as he chooses.

FIRST NIGHT IN HIS NEW HOME

So much has happened in your Border Collie puppy's first day away from the breeder. He's had his first car ride to his new home. He's met his new human family and perhaps the other family pets. He has explored his new house and yard, at least those places where he is to be allowed during his first weeks at home. He may have visited his new veterinarian. He has eaten his first meal or two away from his dam and littermates. Surely that's enough to tire out an eight-week-old Border Collie pup...or so you hope!

It's bedtime. During the day, the pup investigated his crate, which is his new den and sleeping space, so it is not entirely strange to him. Line the crate with a soft towel or blanket that he can snuggle into and gently place him into the crate for the night. Some breeders send home a piece of bedding from where the pup slept with his littermates, and those familiar scents are a great comfort for the puppy on his first night without his siblings.

He will probably whine or cry. The puppy is objecting to the confinement and the fact that he is alone for the first time. This can be a stressful time for you as well as for the pup. It's important that you remain strong and don't let the puppy out of his crate to comfort him. He will fall asleep eventually. If you release him, the puppy will learn that crying means "out" and will continue that habit. You are laying the groundwork for future habits. Some breeders find that soft music can soothe a crying pup and help him get to sleep.

SOCIALIZING YOUR PUPPY

The next 20 weeks of your Border Collie puppy's life are the most important of his entire lifetime. A properly socialized puppy will grow up to be a confident and stable adult who will be a pleasure to live with and a welcome addition to the neighborhood.

The importance of socialization cannot be overemphasized. Research on canine behavior has proven that puppies who are not exposed to new sights, sounds, people and animals during their first 20 weeks of life will grow up to be timid and fearful, even aggressive, and unable to flourish outside of their home environment.

MEET AND MINGLE

Puppies need to meet people and see the world if they are to grow up confident and unafraid. Take your puppy with you on everyday outings and errands. On-lead walks around the neighborhood and to the park offer the pup good exposure to the goings-on of his new human world. Avoid areas frequented by other dogs until your puppy has had his full round of puppy shots; ask your vet when your pup will be properly protected. Arrange for your puppy to meet new people of all ages every week.

Socializing your puppy is not difficult and, in fact, will be a fun time for you both. Lead training goes hand in hand with socialization, so your puppy will be learning how to walk on a lead at the same time that he's meeting the neighborhood. Because the Border Collie is such a terrific breed, your puppy will enjoy being "the new kid on the block." Take him for short walks, to the park and to other dog-friendly places where he will encounter new people, especially children. Puppies automatically recognize children as "little people" and are drawn to play with them. Just make sure that you supervise these meetings and that the children do not get too rough or encourage him to play too hard. An overzealous pup can often nip too hard, frightening the child and in turn making the puppy overly excited. A bad experience in puppyhood can impact a dog for life, so a pup that has a negative experience with a child may grow up to be shy or even aggressive around children.

Take your puppy along on your daily errands. Puppies are natural "people magnets," and most people who see your pup will want to pet him. All of these encounters will help to mold him into a confident adult dog. Likewise, you will soon feel like a confident, responsible dog owner, rightly proud of your handsome Border Collie.

Be especially careful of your puppy's encounters and experiences during the eight-to-ten-week-old period, which is also called the "fear period." This is a serious imprinting period, and all contact during this time should be gentle and positive. A frightening or negative event could leave a permanent impression that could affect his future behavior if a similar situation arises.

Also make sure that your puppy has received his first and second rounds of vaccinations before you expose him to other dogs or bring him to places that other dogs may frequent. Avoid dog parks and other strange-dog areas until your vet assures you that your puppy is fully immunized and resistant to the diseases that can be passed between canines. Discuss socialization with your breeder, as some breeders recommend socializing the puppy even before he has received all of his inoculations, depending on how outgoing the puppy may be.

THE CRITICAL SOCIALIZATION PERIOD

Canine research has shown that a puppy's 8th through 16th week is the most critical learning period of his life. This is when the puppy "learns to learn," a time when he needs positive experiences to build confidence and stability. Puppies who are not exposed to different people and situations outside the home during this period can grow up to be fearful and sometimes aggressive. This is also the best time for puppy lessons, since he has not yet acquired any bad habits that could undermine his ability to learn.

Selecting your puppy from an irresistible armful like this would be quite a challenge. Who could hope for a nicer trio?

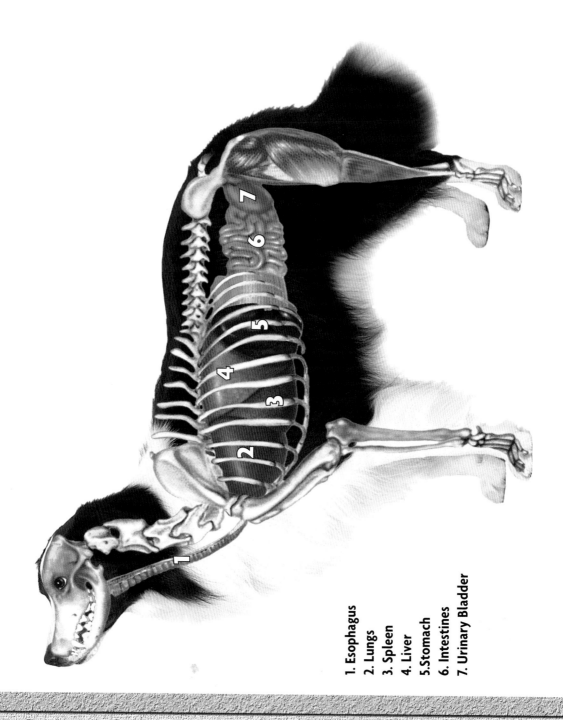

1. Esophagus
2. Lungs
3. Spleen
4. Liver
5.Stomach
6. Intestines
7. Urinary Bladder

INTERNAL ORGANS AND SKELETON OF THE BORDER COLLIE

BORDER COLLIE

Adding a Border Collie to your household means adding a new family member who will need your care each and every day. When your Border Collie pup first comes home, you will start a routine with him so that, as he grows up, your dog will have a daily schedule just as you do. The aspects of your dog's daily care will likewise become regular parts of your day, so you'll both have a new schedule. Dogs learn by consistency and thrive on routine: regular times for meals, exercise, lessons, grooming and potty trips are just as important for your dog as they are to you! Your dog's schedule will depend much on your family's daily routine, but remember that you now have a new member of the family who is a part of your day every day.

FEEDING

Feeding your dog the best diet is based on various factors, including age, activity level, overall condition, size and specifics of the breed. When you visit the breeder, he will share with you his advice about the proper diet for your dog based on his experience with the breed and the foods with which he has had success. Likewise, your vet will be a helpful source of advice throughout the dog's life and will aid you in planning a diet for optimal health.

FEEDING THE PUPPY

Of course, your pup's very first food will be his dam's milk. There may be special situations in which pups fail to nurse, necessitating that the breeder hand-feed

VARIETY IS THE SPICE

Although dog-food manufacturers contend that dogs don't like variety in their diets, studies show quite the opposite to be true. Dogs would much rather vary their meals than eat the same old chow day in and day out. Dry kibble is no more exciting for a dog than the same bowl of bran flakes would be for you. Fortunately, there are dozens of varieties available on the market, and your dog will likely show preference for certain flavors over others. A word of warning: don't overdo it or you'll develop a fussy eater who only prefers chopped beef fillet and asparagus tips every night.

them with a formula, but for the most part pups spend the first weeks of life nursing from their dam. The breeder weans the pups by gradually introducing solid foods and decreasing the milk meals. Pups may even start themselves off on the weaning process, albeit inadvertently, if they snatch bites from their mom's food bowl.

By the time the pups are ready for new homes, they are fully weaned and eating a good puppy food. As a new owner, you may be thinking, "Great! The breeder has taken care of the hard part." Not so fast.

A puppy's first year of life is the time when all or most of his growth and development takes place. This is a delicate time, and diet plays a huge role in proper skeletal and muscular formation. Improper diet and exercise habits can lead to damaging problems that will compromise the dog's health and activity for his entire life. That being said, new owners should not worry needlessly. With the myriad types of food formulated specifically for growing pups of different-sized breeds, dog-food manufacturers have taken much of the guesswork out of feeding your puppy well. Since growth-food formulas are designed to provide the nutrition that a growing puppy needs, it is unnecessary and, in fact, can prove harmful to add supplements to the diet. Research has shown that too

FREE FEEDING
Many owners opt to feed their dogs the free way. That is, they serve dry kibble in a feeder that is available to the dog all day. Arguably, this is the most convenient method of feeding an adult dog, but it may encourage the dog to become fussy about food or defensive over his bowl. Free feeding is an option only for adult dogs, not puppies.

much of certain vitamin supplements and minerals predispose a dog to skeletal problems. It's by no means a case of "if a little is good, a lot is better." At every stage of your dog's life, too much or too little in the way of nutrients can be harmful, which is why a manufactured complete food is the easiest way to know that your dog is getting what he needs.

Because of a young pup's small body and accordingly small digestive system, his daily portion will be divided up into small meals throughout the day. This can mean starting off with three or more meals a day and decreasing the number of meals as the pup matures. Eventually you can feed only one meal a day, although it is generally thought that dividing the day's food into two meals on a morning/evening schedule is healthier for the dog's digestion.

Regarding the feeding schedule, feeding the pup at the same times and in the same place each day is important for both house-breaking purposes and establishing the dog's everyday routine. As for the amount to feed, growing puppies generally need proportionately more food per body weight than their adult counterparts, but a pup should never be allowed to gain excess weight. Dogs of all ages should be kept in proper body condition, but extra weight can strain a pup's developing frame, causing skeletal problems.

Watch your pup's weight as he grows and, if the recommended amounts seem to be too much or too little for your pup, consult the vet about appropriate dietary changes. Keep in mind that treats, although small, can quickly add up throughout the day, contributing unnecessary calories. Treats are fine when used prudently; opt for dog treats specially formulated to be healthy or for nutritious snacks like small pieces of cheese or cooked chicken.

FEEDING THE ADULT DOG

For the adult (meaning physically mature) dog, feeding properly is about maintenance, not growth. Again, correct weight is a concern. Your dog should appear fit and should have an evident "waist." His ribs should not be protruding (a sign of being underweight), but they should be covered by only a slight layer of fat. Under normal circumstances, an adult dog can be maintained

FRESH OPTIONS

While a packaged dog food, formulated to provide complete nutrition and proper balance is no doubt the most convenient way to feed your dog well, some owners prefer to take their dogs' food preparation into their own hands (and kitchens). Homemade fresh-food diets and raw-food diets certainly have their proponents in the dog world. Those who feed the raw, natural diet of the wild do not believe that a dog's food should be cooked and that dogs should not be fed grains of any type. They feel that raw-food diets keep their dogs in optimal physical and temperamental shape, with wonderfully healthy coats and no allergy problems. Those who cook for their dogs typically do so because they do not like the additives and preservatives that go into commercial foods. Many homemade diets are based on a balance of cooked meat, vegetables and grains. If you choose to create your dog's diet on your own, you must thoroughly educate yourself about how to do this correctly for proper nutrition. Not all vets are knowledgeable about these feeding methods, nor will all vets recommend them, so it's best to talk with those vets, breeders, nutrition experts and owners who are experienced and have been successful with fresh- or raw-food diets in dogs.

fairly easily with a high-quality nutritionally complete adult-formula food.

Factor treats into your dog's overall daily caloric intake, and avoid offering table scraps. Overweight dogs are more prone to health problems. Research has even shown that obesity takes years off a dog's life. With that in mind, resist the urge to overfeed

FEEDING WORKING DOGS

The more a dog does, the more he needs to eat! Examples of dogs with higher nutrient requirements are dogs who are very active in training for or competing in sporting disciplines and dogs that are used in a working capacity such as herding or hunting. They do not need supplementation to their regular food; rather, because they need larger amounts of all nutrients, they will need their maintenance food in larger portions. Also ask your vet about specially formulated "performance" diets for active dogs.

When feeding an active dog, it is essential to provide adequate periods of rest before and after eating to avoid stomach upset or the more serious gastric torsion, which can be fatal. Treats can be fed during rest periods as well to keep up the dog's energy in between meals, with plenty of water given. The dog needs time to settle down before and after any eating or drinking, so breaks should be factored into the training program or work routine.

and over-treat. Don't make unnecessary additions to your dog's diet, whether with tidbits or with extra vitamins and minerals.

The amount of food needed for proper maintenance will vary depending on the individual dog's activity level, but you will be able to tell whether the daily portions are keeping him in good shape. With the wide variety of good complete foods available, choosing what to feed is largely a matter of personal preference. Just as with the puppy, the adult dog should have consistency in his mealtimes and feeding place. In addition to a consistent routine, regular mealtimes also allow the owner to see how much his dog is eating. If the dog seems never to be satisfied or, likewise, becomes uninterested in his food, the owner will know right away that something is wrong and can consult the vet.

Don't Forget the Water!

For a dog, it's always time for a drink! Regardless of what type of food he eats, there's no doubt that he needs plenty of water. Fresh cold water, in a clean bowl, should be freely available to your dog at all times. There are special circumstances, such as during puppy housebreaking, when you will want to monitor your pup's water intake so that you will be able to predict when he will need to relieve himself, but water must be available to him nonetheless. Water is essential for hydration and proper body function just as it is in humans.

You will get to know how much your dog typically drinks in a day. Of course, in the heat or if exercising vigorously, he will be more thirsty and will drink more. However, if he begins to drink noticeably more water for no apparent reason, this could signal any of various problems, and you are advised to consult your vet.

Water is the best drink for dogs. Some owners are tempted to give milk from time to time or to moisten dry food with milk, but dogs do not have the enzymes necessary to digest the lactose in milk, which is much different from the milk that nursing

Border Collies require more exercise than average dogs. While not all Border Collies will welcome a swim in a stream, many will enjoy it.

puppies receive. Therefore stick with clean fresh water to quench your dog's thirst, and always have it readily available to him.

GROOMING
BRUSHING

For both the smooth and rough dog, a natural bristle brush can be used for regular routine brushing. A hound glove works nicely on the smooth Border Collie. Regular brushing is effective for removing

Border Collies are naturally active dogs that require a great deal of exercise to maintain their health and sound bodies.

Your Border Collie should be given at least a five-minute brushing every day. This daily contact reinforces the human-dog bonding process.

dead hair and stimulating the dog's natural oils to add shine and a healthy look to the coat. A Border Collie with a short or medium-length coat will require only a five-minute once-over to keep it looking its shiny best. Regular grooming sessions are also a good way to spend time with your dog. Many dogs grow to like the feel of being brushed and will enjoy the routine.

Rough Border Collies with longer, fuller coats will require a bit more attention, especially when they are casting their coats. Mats can form at the base of the ear and on the legs if the dog is not brushed every day or every other day.

Your Border Collie requires a thorough pre-bath brushing to detangle the coat before wetting it.

BATHING

In general, dogs need to be bathed only a few times a year, possibly more often if your dog gets into something messy or if he starts to smell like a dog. Show dogs are usually bathed before every show, which could be as frequent as weekly, although this depends on the owner. Bathing too frequently can have negative effects on the skin and coat, removing natural oils and causing dryness.

If you give your dog his first bath when he is young, he will become accustomed to the process. Wrestling a dog into the tub or chasing a freshly sham- pooed dog who has escaped from the bath will be no fun! Most dogs don't naturally enjoy their baths, but you at least want yours to cooperate with you.

Before bathing the dog, have the items you'll need close at hand. First, decide where you will bathe the dog. You should have a tub with a non-slip surface. Puppies can be bathed in a sink or basin. In warm weather, some like to use a portable pool in the yard, although you'll want to make sure your dog doesn't head for the nearest dirt pile following his bath! You will also need a hose or shower spray to wet the coat thor- oughly, a shampoo formulated for dogs, absorbent towels and perhaps a blow dryer. Human shampoos are too harsh for dogs' coats and will dry them out.

Before wetting the dog, give him a brush-through to remove any dead hair, dirt and mats. Make sure he is at ease in the bath and have the water at a comfortable temperature. Begin bathing by wetting the coat all the way down to the skin. Massage in the shampoo, keeping it away from his face and eyes. Rinse him thoroughly, again avoiding the eyes and ears, as you don't want to get water into the ear canals. A thorough rinsing is important, as shampoo residue is drying and itchy to the dog. After rinsing, wrap him in a towel to absorb the initial moisture. You can finish drying with either a towel or a blow dryer on low heat, held at a safe distance from the dog. You should keep the dog indoors and away from drafts until he is completely dry.

Ear Cleaning

While keeping your dog's ears clean unfortunately will not cause him to "hear" your commands any better, it will protect him from ear infection and ear-mite

WATER SHORTAGE

No matter how well behaved your dog is, bathing is always a project! Nothing can substitute for a good warm bath, but owners do have the option of giving their dogs "dry" baths. Pet shops sell excellent products, in both powder and spray forms, designed for spot-cleaning your dog. These dry shampoos are convenient for touch-up jobs when you don't have the time to bathe your dog in the traditional way.

Muddy feet, messy behinds and smelly coats can be spot-cleaned and deodorized with a "wet-nap"-style cleaner. On those days when your dog insists on rolling in fresh goose droppings and there's no time for a bath, a spot bath can save the day. These pre-moistened wipes are also handy for other grooming needs like wiping faces, ears and eyes and freshening tails and behinds.

infestation. In addition, a dog's ears are vulnerable to waxy build-up and to collecting foreign matter from the outdoors. Look in your dog's ears regularly to ensure that they look pink, clean and

After your Border Collie has been bathed and dried, the coat should be combed thoroughly.

otherwise healthy. Even if they look fine, an odor in the ears signals a problem and means it's time to call the vet.

A dog's ears should be cleaned regularly; once a week is suggested, and you can do this along with your regular brushing. Using a cotton ball or pad, wipe the ear gently. Never probe into the ear canal. You can use an ear-cleansing liquid or powder available from your vet or pet-supply store; alternatively, you might prefer to use home-made solutions with ingredients like one part white vinegar and one part hydrogen peroxide. Ask your vet

about home remedies before you attempt to concoct something on your own.

Keep your dog's ears free of excess hair by plucking it as needed. If done gently, this will be painless for the dog. Look for wax, brown droppings (a sign of ear mites), redness or any other abnormalities. At the first sign of a problem, contact your vet so that he can prescribe an appropriate medication.

NAIL CLIPPING

Having his nails trimmed is not on any dog's list of favorite things to do. With this in mind, you will

THE EARS KNOW

Examining your puppy's ears helps ensure good internal health. The ears are the eyes to the dog's innards! Begin handling your puppy's ears when he's still young so that he doesn't protest every time you lift a flap or touch his ears. Yeast and bacteria are two of the culprits that you can detect by examining the ear. You will notice a strong, often foul, odor, debris, redness or some kind of discharge. All of these point to health problems that can worsen over time. Additionally, you are on the lookout for wax accumulation, ear mites and other tiny bothersome parasites and their even tinier droppings. You may have to pluck hair with tweezers in order to have a better view into the dog's ears, but this is painless if done carefully.

need to accustom your puppy to the procedure at a young age so that he will sit still for his pedicures. Long nails can cause the dog's feet to spread, which is not good for him; likewise, long nails can hurt if they unintentionally scratch, not good for you.

Some dogs' nails are worn down naturally by regular walking on hard surfaces, so the frequency with which you clip depends on your individual dog. Look at his nails from time to time and clip as needed; a good way to know when it's time for a trim is if you hear your dog clicking as he walks across the floor.

There are several types of nail clippers and even electric nail-grinding tools made for dogs; first we'll discuss using the clipper. To start, have your clipper ready and some doggie treats on hand. You want your pup to view his nail-clipping sessions in a positive light, and what better way to convince him than with food? You may want to enlist the help of an assistant to comfort the pup and offer treats as you concentrate on the clipping itself. The guillotine-type clipper is thought of by many as the easiest type to use; the nail tip is inserted into the opening, and blades on the top and bottom snip it off in one clip.

Start by grasping the pup's paw; a little pressure on the foot pad causes the nail to extend, making it easier to clip. Clip off a

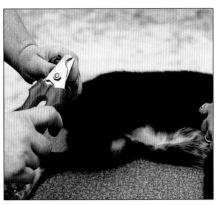

Your local pet shop sells nail clippers especially made for dogs' nails. The guillotine-type is the most preferred.

little at a time. If you can see the "quick," which is a blood vessel that runs through each nail, you will know how much to trim, as you do not want to cut into the quick. On that note, if you do cut the quick, which will cause bleeding, you can stem the flow of blood with a styptic pencil or other clotting agent. If you mistakenly nip the quick, do not panic or fuss, as this will cause the pup to be afraid. Simply reassure the pup, stop the bleeding and move on to the next nail. Don't be discouraged; you will become a professional canine pedicurist with practice.

You may or may not be able to see the quick, so it's best to just clip off a small bit at a time. The dark dot in the center of the nail is the quick, which is your cue to stop clipping. Tell the puppy he's a "good boy" and offer a piece of treat with each clipped nail. You can also use nail-clipping time to examine the footpads, making

You can use trimming scissors to cut away the excess hair growth on the foot to keep it looking tidy.

sure that they are not dry and cracked and that nothing has become embedded in them.

The nail grinder, the second option, is many owners' first choice. Accustoming the puppy to the sound of the grinder and sensation of the buzz presents fewer challenges than the clipper, and there's no chance of cutting through the quick. Use the grinder on a low setting and always talk soothingly to your dog. He won't mind his salon visit, and he'll have nicely polished nails as well.

A CLEAN SMILE

The standard calls for a perfect scissors bite with the upper teeth closely overlapping the lower teeth.

Another essential part of grooming is brushing your dog's teeth and checking his overall oral condition. Studies show that around 80% of dogs experience dental problems by two years of age, and the percentage is higher in older dogs. Therefore it is likely that your dog will have trouble with his teeth and gums unless you are proactive with home dental care.

The most common dental problem in dogs is plaque build-up. If not treated, this causes gum disease, infection and resultant tooth loss. Bacteria from these infections spread throughout the body, affecting the vital organs. Do you need much more convincing to start brushing your dog's teeth? If so, take a good whiff of your dog's breath, and read on.

Fortunately, home dental care is rather easy and convenient for pet owners. Specially formulated canine toothpaste is easy to find in pet shops. You should use one of these toothpastes, not a product for humans. Some doggie pastes are even available in flavors appealing to dogs. If your dog likes the flavor, he will tolerate the process better, making things much easier for you. Doggie toothbrushes come in different sizes and are designed to fit the contour of a canine mouth. Rubber fingertip brushes fit right on one of your fingers and have rubber nodes to

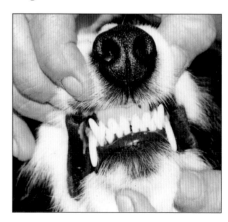

clean the teeth and massage the gums. This may be easier to handle, as it is akin to rubbing your dog's teeth with your finger.

As with other grooming tasks, accustom your Border Collie pup to his dental care early on. Start gently, for a few minutes at a time, so that he gets used to the feel of the brush and to your handling his mouth. Offer praise and petting so that he looks at tooth-care time as a time when he gets extra love and attention. The routine should become second nature; he may not like it, but he should at least tolerate it.

Aside from brushing, offer dental toys to your dog and feed crunchy biscuits, which help to minimize plaque. Rope toys have the added benefit of acting like floss as the dog chews. At your adult dog's yearly check-ups, the vet will likely perform a thorough tooth scraping as well as a complete check for any problems. Proper care of your dog's teeth will ensure that you will enjoy your dog's smile for many years to come. The next time your dog goes to give you a hello kiss, you'll be glad you spent the time caring for his teeth.

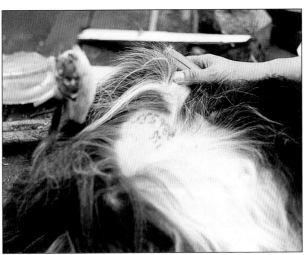

A tattoo is usually done in a relatively hair-free spot such as the inside of the hind leg.

IDENTIFICATION AND TRAVEL

ID FOR YOUR DOG

You love your Border Collie and want to keep him safe. Of course you take every precaution to prevent his escaping from the yard or becoming lost or stolen. You have a sturdy high fence and you always keep your dog on lead when out and about in public places. If your dog is not properly identified, however, you are over-looking a major aspect of his safety.

There are several ways to identify your dog. First, the tradi-tional dog tag should be a staple in your dog's wardrobe, attached to his everyday collar. Tags can be made of sturdy plastic and vari-ous metals and should include your contact information so that a person who finds the dog can get in touch with you right away to

Playtime! The puppies have been tattooed for identification purposes (enhanced for this photograph). Some breeders have the whole litter tattooed as early as six or eight weeks.

arrange his return. Of course, it is important that the tag stays on the collar, so have a secure "O" ring attachment; you also can explore the type of tag that slides right onto the collar.

In addition to the ID tag, which every dog should wear even if identified by another method, two other forms of identification have become popular: microchipping and tattooing. In microchipping, a tiny scannable chip is painlessly inserted under the dog's skin. The number is registered to you so that, if your lost dog turns up at a clinic or shelter, the chip can be scanned to retrieve your contact information.

The advantage of the microchip is that it is a permanent form of ID, but there are some factors to consider. Several different companies make microchips, and not all are compatible with the others' scanning devices. It's best to find a company with a universal microchip that can be read by

scanners made by other companies as well. It won't do any good to have the dog chipped if the information cannot be retrieved. Also, not every humane society, shelter and clinic is equipped with a scanner, although more and more facilities are equipping themselves. In fact, many shelters microchip dogs that they adopt out to new homes.

Because the microchip is not visible to the eye, the dog must wear a tag that states that he is microchipped so that whoever picks him up will know to have him scanned. He of course also should have a tag with contact information in case his chip cannot be read. Humane societies and veterinary clinics offer this service, which is usually very affordable.

Though less popular than microchipping, tattooing is another permanent method of ID for dogs. Most vets perform this service, and there are also clinics that perform dog tattooing. This is also an affordable procedure and one that will not cause much discomfort for the dog.

To ensure that the tattoo is effective in aiding your dog's return to you, the tattoo number must be registered with a national organization. That way, when someone finds a tattooed dog a phone call to the registry will quickly match the dog with his owner.

HIT THE ROAD

Car travel with your Border Collie may be limited to necessity only, such as trips to the vet, or you may bring your dog along almost everywhere you go. This will depend much on your individual dog and how he reacts to rides in the car. You can begin desensitizing your dog to car travel as a pup so that it's something that he's used to. Still, some dogs suffer from motion sickness. Your vet may prescribe a medication for this if trips in the car pose a problem for your dog. At the very least, you will need to get him to the vet, so he will need to tolerate these trips with the least amount of hassle possible.

Start taking your pup on short trips, maybe just around the block to start. If he is fine with short trips, lengthen your rides a little at a time. Start to take him on your errands or just for drives around town. By this time it will be easy to tell whether your dog is a born traveler or would prefer staying at home when you are on the road.

Of course, safety is a concern for dogs in the car. First, he must travel securely, not left loose to roam about the car where he could be injured or distract the driver. A young pup can be held by a passenger initially but should soon graduate to a travel crate, which can be the same

Dogs, during any mode of travel, should be restrained. During a car ride, Border Collies are safer in their individual crates.

crate he uses in the home. Other options include a car harness (like a seat belt for dogs) and partitioning the back of the car with a gate made for this purpose.

Bring along what you will need for the dog. He should wear his collar and ID tags, of course, and you should bring his leash, water (and food if a long trip) and clean-up materials for potty breaks and in case of motion sickness. Always keep your dog on his leash when you make stops, and never leave him alone in the car. Many a dog has died from the heat inside a closed car; this does not take much time at all. A dog left alone inside a car can also be a target for thieves.

TRAINING YOUR
BORDER COLLIE

Here's a Border Collie "sponge" ready to soak up every lesson you pour.

BASIC TRAINING PRINCIPLES: PUPPY VS. ADULT

There's a big difference between training an adult dog and training a young puppy. With a young puppy, everything is new. At eight to ten weeks of age, he will be experiencing many things, and he has nothing with which to compare these experiences. Up to this point, he has been with his dam and littermates, not one-on-one with people except in his interactions with his breeder and visitors to the litter.

BASIC PRINCIPLES OF DOG TRAINING

1. Start training early. A young puppy is ready, willing and able.
2. Timing is your all-important tool. Praise at the exact time that the dog responds correctly. Pay close attention.
3. Patience is almost as important as timing!
4. Repeat! The same word has to mean the same thing every time.
5. In the beginning, praise all correct behavior verbally, along with treats and petting.

When you first bring the puppy home, he is eager to please you. This means that he accepts doing things your way. During the next couple of months, he will absorb the basis of everything he needs to know for the rest of his life. This early age is even referred to as the "sponge" stage. After that, for the next 18 months, it's up to you to reinforce good manners by building on the foundation that you've established. Once your puppy is reliable in basic commands and behavior and has reached the appropriate age, you may gradually introduce him to some of the interesting sports, games and activities available to pet owners and their dogs.

Raising your puppy is a family affair. Each member of the family must know what rules to set forth for the puppy and how to use the same one-word commands to mean exactly the same thing every time. Even if yours is a large family, one person will soon be considered by the pup to be the leader, the Alpha person in his pack, the "boss" who must be obeyed. Often that highly regarded person turns out to be the one who feeds the puppy. Food ranks very high on the puppy's list of important things! That's why your puppy is rewarded with small treats along with verbal praise when he responds to you correctly. As the puppy learns to do what you want him to do, the food rewards are gradually eliminated and only the praise remains. If you were to keep up with the food treats, you could have two problems on your hands—an obese dog and a beggar.

Training begins the minute your Border Collie puppy steps through the doorway of your home, so don't make the mistake of putting the puppy on the floor and telling him by your actions to "Go for it! Run wild!" Even if this is your first puppy, you must act as if you know what you're doing: be the boss. An uncertain pup may be terrified to move, while a bold one will be ready to take you at your word and start plotting to destroy the house! Before you collected your puppy, you decided where his own special place would be, and that's where to put him when

Border Collies derived from working-dog stock, as opposed to show-dog stock, are more likely to demonstrate an early aptitude for herding trials.

KIDS RULE

Children of 10 to 12 year of age are old enough to understand the "be kind to dumb animals" approach and will have fun training their dogs, especially to do tricks. It teaches them to be tolerant, patient and appreciative as well as to accept failure to some extent. Young children can be tyrants, making unreasonable demands on the dog and unable to cope with defeat, blaming it all on the dog. Toddlers need not apply.

you first arrive home. Give him a house tour after he has investigated his area and had a nap and a bathroom "pit stop."

It's worth mentioning here that, if you've adopted an adult dog that is completely trained to your liking, lucky you! You're off the hook! However, if that dog spent his life up to this point in a kennel, or even in a good home but without any real training, be prepared to tackle the job ahead. A dog three years of age or older with no previous training cannot be blamed for not knowing what he was never taught. While the dog is trying to understand and learn your rules, at the same time he has to unlearn many of his previously self-taught habits and general view of the world.

Working with a professional trainer will speed up your progress with an adopted adult dog. You'll need patience, too. Some new rules may be close to impossible for the dog to accept. After all, he's been successful so far by doing everything his way! (Patience again.) He may agree with your instruction for a few days and then slip back into his old ways, so you must be just as consistent and understanding in your teaching as you would be with a puppy. (More patience needed yet again!) Your dog has to learn to pay attention to your voice, your family, the daily routine, new smells, new sounds and, in some cases, even a new climate.

One of the most important things to find out about a newly adopted adult dog is his reaction to children (yours and others), strangers and your friends, and how he acts upon meeting other dogs. If he was not socialized with dogs as a puppy, this could be a major problem. This does not mean that he's a "bad" dog, a vicious dog or an aggressive dog; rather, it means that he has no idea how to read another dog's body language. There's no way for him to tell whether the other dog is a friend or foe. Survival instinct takes over, telling him to attack first and ask questions later. This definitely calls for professional help and, even then, may not be a behavior that can be corrected 100% reliably (or even at all). If you have a puppy, this is why it is so very important to introduce your young puppy properly to other puppies and "dog-friendly" adult dogs.

HOUSE-TRAINING YOUR BORDER COLLIE

Dogs are tactility-oriented when it comes to house-training. In other words, they respond to the surface on which they are given approval to eliminate. The choice is yours (the dog's version is in parentheses): The lawn (including the neighbors' lawns)? A bare patch of earth under a tree (where people like to sit and relax in the summertime)? Concrete steps or patio (all sidewalks, garage and basement floors)? The curbside (watch out for cars)? A small area of crushed stone in a corner of the yard (mine!)? The latter is the best choice if you can manage it, because it will remain strictly for the dog's use and is easy to keep clean.

You can start out with paper-training indoors and switch over to an outdoor surface as the puppy matures and gains control over his need to eliminate. For

A well-socialized adult dog knows the ins and outs of the doggy pack. Although every dog is different, socialization makes a dog trainable and reliable.

the nay-sayers, don't worry—this won't mean that the dog will soil on every piece of newspaper lying around the house. You are training him to go outside, remember? Starting out by paper-training often is the only choice for a city dog.

WHEN YOUR PUPPY'S "GOT TO GO"
Your puppy's need to relieve himself is seemingly non-stop, but signs of improvement will be seen each week. From 8 to 10 weeks old, the puppy will have to be taken outside every time he wakes up, about 10-15 minutes after every meal and after every period of play—all day long, from first thing in the morning until his

bedtime! That's a total of ten or more trips per day to teach the puppy where it's okay to relieve himself. With that schedule in mind, you can see that house-training a young puppy is not a part-time job. It requires someone to be home all day.

If that seems overwhelming or impossible, do a little planning. For example, plan to pick up your puppy at the start of a vacation period. If you can't get home in the middle of the day, plan to hire a dog-sitter or ask a neighbor to come over to take the pup outside, feed him his lunch and then take him out again about ten or so minutes after he's eaten. Also make arrangements with that or another person to be your "emergency" contact if you have to stay late on the job. Remind yourself—repeat-edly—that this hectic schedule improves as the puppy gets older.

HOME WITHIN A HOME
Your Border Collie puppy needs to be confined to one secure, puppy-proof area when no one is able to watch his every move. Generally the kitchen is the place of choice because the floor is washable. Likewise, it's a busy family area that will accustom the pup to a variety of noises, everything from pots and pans to the telephone, blender and dishwasher. He will also be enchanted by the smell of your cooking (and will never be critical

---

POTTY COMMAND

Most dogs love to please their masters; there are no bounds to what dogs will do to make their owners happy. The potty command is a good example of this theory. If toileting on command makes the master happy, then more power to him. Puppies will obligingly piddle if it really makes their keepers smile. Some owners can be creative about which word they will use to command their dogs to relieve themselves. Some popular choices are "Potty," "Tinkle," "Piddle," "Let's go," "Hurry up" and "Toilet." Give the command every time your puppy goes into position and the puppy will begin to associate his business with the command.

height on the side of the ex-pen so it won't become a splashing pool for an innovative puppy. His food dish can go on the floor, near but not under the water bowl.

Crates are something that pet owners are at last getting used to for their dogs. Wild or domestic canines have always preferred to sleep in den-like safe spots, and that is exactly what the crate provides. How often have you seen adult dogs that choose to sleep under a table or chair even though they have full run of the house? It's the den connection.

In your "happy" voice, use the word "Crate" every time you put the pup into his den. If he's new to a crate, toss in a small biscuit for him to chase the first few

Part of "control" means limiting access to any areas in your home and yard that may be dangerous for your Border Collie.

when you burn something). An exercise pen (also called an "ex-pen," a puppy version of a playpen) within the room of choice is an excellent means of confinement for a young pup. He can see out and has a certain amount of space in which to run about, but he is safe from dangerous things like electrical cords, heating units, trash baskets or open kitchen-supply cabinets. Place the pen where the puppy will not get a blast of heat or air conditioning.

In the pen, you can put a few toys, his bed (which can be his crate if the dimensions of pen and crate are compatible) and a few layers of newspaper in one small corner, just in case. A water bowl can be hung at a convenient

---

DAILY SCHEDULE

How many relief trips does your puppy need per day? A puppy up to the age of 14 weeks will need to go outside about 8 to 12 times per day! You will have to take the pup out any time he starts sniffing around the floor or turning in small circles, as well as after naps, meals, games and lessons or whenever he's released from his crate. Once the puppy is 14 to 22 weeks of age, he will require only 6 to 8 relief trips. At the ages of 22 to 32 weeks, the puppy will require about 5 to 7 trips. Adult dogs typically require 4 relief trips per day, in the morning, afternoon, evening and late at night.

Experienced breeders introduce puppies to the crate as a part of their daily routine. Border Collie pups instinctively take to crates.

replace his mother's heartbeat, or a hot-water bottle to replace her warmth, are just that—old ideas. The clock could drive the puppy nuts, and the hot-water bottle could end up as a very soggy waterbed! An extremely good breeder would have introduced your puppy to the crate by letting two pups sleep together for a couple of nights, followed by several nights alone. How thankful you will be if you found that breeder!

Safe toys in the pup's crate or area will keep him occupied, but monitor their condition closely. Discard any toys that show signs of being chewed to bits. Squeaky parts, bits of stuffing or plastic or

times. At night, after he's been outside, he should sleep in his crate. The crate may be kept in his designated area at night or, if you want to be sure to hear those wake-up yips in the morning, put the crate in a corner of your bedroom. However, don't make any response whatsoever to whining or crying. If he's completely ignored, he'll settle down and get to sleep.

Good bedding for a young puppy is an old folded bath towel or an old blanket, something that is easily washable and disposable if necessary ("accidents" will happen!). Never put newspaper in the puppy's crate. Also those old ideas about adding a clock to

TIDY BOY

Clean by nature, dogs do not like to soil their dens, which in effect are their crates or sleeping quarters. Unless not feeling well, dogs will not defecate or urinate in their crates. Crate training capitalizes on the dog's natural desire to keep his den clean. Be conscientious about giving the puppy as many opportunities to relieve himself outdoors as possible. Reward the puppy for correct behavior. Praise him and pat him whenever he "goes" in the correct location. Even the tidiest of puppies can have potty accidents, so be patient and dedicate more energy to helping your puppy achieve a clean lifestyle.

any other small pieces can cause intestinal blockage or possibly choking if swallowed.

PROGRESSING WITH POTTY-TRAINING

After you've taken your puppy out and he has relieved himself in the area you've selected, he can have some free time with the family as long as there is someone responsible for watching him. That doesn't mean just someone in the same room who is watching TV or busy on the computer, but one person who is doing nothing other than keeping an eye on the pup, playing with him on the floor and helping him understand his position in the pack.

This first taste of freedom will let you begin to set the house rules. If you don't want the dog on the furniture, now is the time to prevent his first attempts to jump up onto the couch. The word to use in this case is "Off," not "Down." "Down" is the word you will use to teach the down position, which is something entirely different.

Most corrections at this stage come in the form of simply distracting the puppy. Instead of telling him "No" for "Don't chew the carpet," distract the chomping puppy with a toy and he'll forget about the carpet.

As you are playing with the pup, do not forget to watch him closely and pay attention to his body language. Whenever you see him begin to circle or sniff, take the puppy outside to relieve himself. If you are paper-training, put him back into his confined area on the newspapers. In either case, praise him as he eliminates while he actually is in the act of relieving himself. Three seconds after he has finished is too late! You'll be praising him for running toward you, or picking up a toy or whatever he may be doing at that moment, and that's not what you want to be praising him for. Timing is a vital tool in all dog training. Use it!

Remove soiled newspapers immediately and replace them with clean ones. You may want to take a small piece of soiled paper

Your Border Collie puppy will soon regard his crate as his den-away-from-home. Do not leave food or water in the dog's crate.

and place it in the middle of the new clean papers, as the scent will attract him to that spot when it's time to go again. That scent attraction is why it's so important to clean up any messes made in the house by using a product specially made to eliminate the odor of dog urine and droppings. Regular household cleansers won't do the trick. Pet shops sell the best pet deodorizers. Invest in the largest container you can find.

Scent attraction eventually will lead your pup to his chosen spot outdoors; this is the basis of outdoor training. When you take your puppy outside to relieve

EXTRA! EXTRA!
The headlines read: "Puppy Piddles Here!" Breeders commonly use newspapers to line their whelping pens, so puppies learn to associate newspapers with relieving themselves. Do not use newspapers to line your pup's crate, as this will signal to your puppy that it is OK to urinate in his crate. If you choose to paper-train your puppy, you will layer newspapers on a section of the floor near the door he uses to go outside. You should encourage the puppy to use the papers to relieve himself, and bring him there whenever you see him getting ready to go. Little by little, you will reduce the size of the newspaper-covered area so that the puppy will learn to relieve himself "on the other side of the door."

himself, use a one-word command such as "Outside" or "Go-potty" (that's one word to the puppy!) as you pick him up and attach his leash. Then put him down in his area. If for any reason you can't carry him, snap the leash on quickly and lead him to his spot. Now comes the hard part—hard for you, that is. Just stand there until he urinates and defecates. Move him a few feet in one direction or another if he's just sitting there looking at you, but remember that this is neither playtime nor time for a walk. This is strictly a business trip! Then, as he circles and squats (remember your timing!), give him a quiet "Good dog" as praise. If you start to jump for joy, ecstatic over his performance, he'll do one of two things: either he will stop midstream, as it were, or he'll do it again for you—in the house—and expect you to be just as delighted!

Give him five minutes or so and, if he doesn't go in that time, take him back indoors to his confined area and try again in another ten minutes, or immediately if you see him sniffing and circling. By careful observation, you'll soon work out a successful schedule.

Accidents, by the way, are just that—accidents. Clean them up quickly and thoroughly, without comment, after the puppy has been taken outside to finish his business and then put back into his area or crate. If you witness an accident in progress, say "No!" in a stern voice and get the pup outdoors immediately. No punishment is needed. You and your puppy are just learning each other's language, and sometimes it's easy to miss a puppy's message. Chalk it up to experience and watch more closely from now on.

KEEPING THE PACK ORDERLY

Discipline is a form of training that brings order to life. For example, military discipline is what allows the soldiers in an army to work as one. Discipline is a form of teaching and, in dogs, is the basis of how the successful pack operates. Each member knows his place in the pack and all respect the leader, or Alpha dog. It is essential for your puppy that you establish this type of relationship,

BOOT CAMP

Even if one member of the family assumes the role of "drill sergeant," every other member of the family has to know what's involved in the dog's education. Success depends on consistency and knowing what words to use, how to use them, how to say them, when to say them and, most important to the dog, how to praise. The dog will be happy to respond to all members of the family, but don't make the little guy think he's in boot camp!

with you as the Alpha, or leader. It is a form of social coexistence that all canines recognize and accept. Discipline, therefore, is never to be confused with punishment. When you teach your puppy how you want him to behave, and he behaves properly and you praise him for it, you are disciplining him with a form of positive reinforcement.

For a dog, rewards come in the form of praise, a smile, a cheerful tone of voice, a few friendly pats or a rub of the ears. Rewards are also small food treats. Obviously, that does not mean bits of regular dog food. Instead, treats are very

Another invaluable advantage to crate training presents itself when traveling with your Border Collie. He's ready to go—safe and content.

small bits of special things like cheese or pieces of soft dog treats. The idea is to reward the dog with something very small that he can taste and swallow, providing instant positive reinforcement. If he has to take time to chew the treat, by the time he is finished he will have forgotten what he did to earn it!

Your puppy should never be physically punished. The displeasure shown on your face and in your voice is sufficient to signal to the pup that he has done something wrong. He wants to please everyone higher up on the social ladder, especially his leader, so a scowl and harsh voice will take care of the error. Growling out the word "Shame!" when the pup is caught in the act of doing something wrong is better than the repetitive "No." Some dogs hear "No" so often that they begin to think it's their name! By the way, do not use the dog's name when you're correcting him. His name is reserved to get his attention for something pleasant about to take place.

There are punishments that have nothing to do with you. For example, your dog may think that chasing cats is one reason for his existence. You can try to stop it as much as you like but without success, because it's such fun for the dog. But one good hissing, spitting, swipe of a cat's claws across the dog's nose will put an

LEASH TRAINING

House-training and leash training go hand in hand, literally. When taking your puppy outside to do his business, lead him there on his leash. Unless an emergency potty run is called for, do not whisk the puppy up into your arms and take him outside. If you have a fenced yard, you have the advantage of letting the puppy loose to go out, but it's better to put the dog on the leash and take him to his designated place in the yard until he is reliably house-trained. Taking the puppy for a walk is the best way to house-train a dog. The dog will associate the walk with his time to relieve himself, and the exercise of walking stimulates the dog's bowels and bladder. Dogs that are not trained to relieve themselves on a walk may hold it until they get back home, which of course defeats half the purpose of the walk.

end to the game forever. Intervene only when your dog's eyeball is seriously at risk. Cat scratches can cause permanent damage to an innocent but annoying puppy.

PUPPY KINDERGARTEN

COLLAR AND LEASH

Before you begin your Border Collie puppy's education, he must be used to his collar and leash. Choose a collar for your puppy that is secure, but not heavy or bulky. He won't enjoy training if

Canine Development Schedule

It is important to understand how and at what age a puppy develops into adulthood. If you are a puppy owner, consult the following Canine Development Schedule to determine the stage of development your puppy is currently experiencing. This knowledge will help you as you work with the puppy in the weeks and months ahead.

Period	Age	Characteristics
First to Third	Birth to Seven Weeks	Puppy needs food, sleep and warmth and responds to simple and gentle touching. Needs mother for security and disciplining. Needs littermates for learning and interacting with other dogs. Pup learns to function within a pack and learns pack order of dominance. Begin socializing pup with adults and children for short periods. Pup begins to become aware of his environment.
Fourth	Eight to Twelve Weeks	Brain is fully developed. Pup needs socializing with outside world. Remove from mother and littermates. Needs to change from canine pack to human pack. Human dominance necessary. Fear period occurs between 8 and 12 weeks. Avoid fright and pain.
Fifth	Thirteen to Sixteen Weeks	Training and formal obedience should begin. Less association with other dogs, more with people, places, situations. Period will pass easily if you remember this is pup's change-to-adolescence time. Be firm and fair. Flight instinct prominent. Permissiveness and over-disciplining can do permanent damage. Praise for good behavior.
Juvenile	Four to Eight Months	Another fear period about 7 to 8 months of age. It passes quickly, but be cautious of fright and pain. Sexual maturity reached. Dominant traits established. Dog should understand sit, down, come and stay by now.

Note: These are approximate time frames. Allow for individual differences in puppies.

The collar and leash that you select for your Border Collie should be light-weight but strong and durable.

The collar and leash that you select for your Border Collie should be light-weight but strong and durable.

he's uncomfortable. A flat buckle collar is fine for everyday wear and for initial puppy training. For older dogs, there are several types of training collars such as the martingale, which is a double loop that tightens slightly around the neck, or the head collar, which is similar to a horse's halter. Do not use a chain choke collar unless you have been specifically shown how to put it on and how to use it. You may not be disposed to use a chain choke collar even if your breeder has told you that it's suitable for your Border Collie.

A lightweight 6-foot woven cotton or nylon training leash is preferred by most trainers because it is easy to fold up in your hand and comfortable to hold because there is a certain amount of give to it. There are lessons where the dog will start off 6 feet away from you at the end of the leash. The leash used to take the puppy outside to relieve himself is shorter because you don't want him to roam away from his area. The shorter leash will also be the one to use when you walk the puppy.

If you've been fortunate enough to enroll in a Puppy

Kindergarten training class, suggestions will be made as to the best collar and leash for your young puppy. I say "fortunate" because your puppy will be in a class with puppies in his age range (up to five months old) of all breeds and sizes. It's the perfect way for him to learn the right way (and the wrong way) to interact with other dogs as well as their people. You cannot teach your puppy how to interpret another dog's sign language. For a first-time puppy owner, these socialization classes are invaluable. For experienced dog owners, they are a real boon to further training.

ATTENTION

You've been using the dog's name since the minute you collected him from the breeder, so you should be able to get his attention by saying his name—with a big

"Sit" is a good place to start with your Border Collie's lesson plans.

smile and in an excited tone of voice. His response will be the puppy equivalent of "Here I am! What are we going to do?" Your immediate response (if you haven't guessed by now) is "Good dog." Rewarding him at the moment he pays attention to you teaches him the proper way to respond when he hears his name.

EXERCISES FOR A BASIC CANINE EDUCATION

THE SIT EXERCISE

There are several ways to teach the puppy to sit. The first one is

---

READY, SIT, GO!

On your marks, get set: train! Most professional trainers agree that the sit command is the place to start your dog's formal education. Sitting is a natural posture for most dogs, and they respond to the sit exercise willingly and readily. For every lesson, begin with the sit command so that you start out on a successful note; likewise, you should practice the sit command at the end of every lesson as well, because you always want to end on a high note.

Border Collies are easily trained to sit. Gently assisting the dog into position is an acceptable method. Keep in mind that successful performances should be rewarded with verbal praise.

to catch him whenever he is about to sit and, as his backside nears the floor, say "Sit, good dog!" That's positive reinforcement and, if your timing is sharp, he will learn that what he's doing at that second is connected to your saying "Sit" and that you think he's clever for doing it!

Another method is to start with the puppy on his leash in front of you. Show him a treat in the palm of your right hand. Bring your hand up under his nose and, almost in slow motion, move your hand up and back so his nose goes up in the air and his head tilts back as he follows the treat in your hand. At that point, he will have to either sit or fall over, so as

his back legs buckle under, say "Sit, good dog," and then give him the treat and lots of praise. You may have to begin with your hand lightly running up his chest, actually lifting his chin up until he sits. Some (usually older) dogs require gentle pressure on their hindquarters with the left hand, in which case the dog should be on your left side. Puppies generally do not appreciate this physical dominance.

After a few times, you should be able to show the dog a treat in the open palm of your hand, raise your hand waist-high as you say "Sit" and have him sit. Once again, you have taught him two things at the same time. Both the verbal command and the motion of the hand are signals for the sit. Your puppy is watching you almost more than he is listening to you, so what you do is just as important as what you say.

SIT AROUND THE HOUSE

"Sit" is the command you'll use most often. Your pup objects when placed in a sit with your hands, so try the "bringing the food up under his chin" method. Better still, catch him in the act! Your dog will sit on his own many times throughout the day, so let him know that he's doing the "Sit" by rewarding him. Praise him and have him sit for everything—toys, connecting his leash, his dinner, before going out the door, etc.

Don't save any of these drills only for training sessions. Use them as much as possible at odd times during a normal day. The dog should always sit before being given his food dish. He should sit to let you go through a doorway first, when the doorbell rings or when you stop to speak to someone on the street.

THE DOWN EXERCISE

Before beginning to teach the down command, you must consider how the dog feels about this exercise. To him, "down" is a submissive position. Being flat on the floor with you standing over him is not his idea of fun. It's up to you to let him know that, while it may not be fun, the reward of your approval is worth his effort.

Start with the puppy on your left side in a sit position. Hold the leash right above his collar in your left hand. Have an extra-special treat, such as a small piece of cooked chicken or hot dog, in your right hand. Place it at the end of the pup's nose and steadily move your hand down and forward along the ground. Hold the leash to prevent a sudden lunge for the food. As the puppy goes into the down position, say "Down" very gently.

The difficulty with this exercise is twofold: it's both the submissive aspect and the fact that most people say the word "Down" as if they were a drill sergeant in

DOWN

"Down" is a harsh-sounding word and a submissive posture in dog body language, thus presenting two obstacles in teaching the down command. When the dog is about to flop down on his own, tell him "Good down." Pups that are not good about being handled learn better by having food lowered in front of them. A dog that trusts you can be gently guided into position. When you give the command "Down," be sure to say it sweetly!

charge of recruits! So issue the command sweetly, give him the treat and have the pup maintain the down position for several seconds. If he tries to get up immediately, place your hands on his shoulders and press down gently, giving him a very quiet "Good dog." As you progress with this lesson, increase the "down time"

positions. To teach the sit/stay, have the dog sit on your left side. Hold the leash at waist level in your left hand and let the dog know that you have a treat in your closed right hand. Step forward on your right foot as you say "Stay." Immediately turn and stand directly in front of the dog, keeping your right hand up high so he'll keep his eye on the treat hand and maintain the sit position for a count of five. Return to your original position and offer the reward.

Increase the length of the sit/stay each time until the dog can hold it for at least 30 seconds without moving. After about a week of success, move out on your right foot and take two steps before turning to face the dog. Give the "Stay" hand signal (left palm back toward the dog's head) as you leave. He gets the treat

Once your Border Collie is trained to sit, you can progress to the sit/stay. This is best taught by gradually increasing the length of time of the stay and the distance from the dog.

until he will hold it until you say "Okay" (his cue for release). Practice this one in the house at various times throughout the day.

By increasing the length of time during which the dog must maintain the down position, you'll find many uses for it. For example, he can lie at your feet in the vet's office or anywhere that both of you have to wait, when you are on the phone, while the family is eating and so forth. If you progress to training for competitive obedience, he'll already be all set for the exercise called the "long down."

THE STAY EXERCISE

You can teach your Border Collie to stay in the sit, down and stand

I WILL FOLLOW YOU

Obedience isn't just a classroom activity. In your home you have many great opportunities to teach your dog polite manners. Allowing your pet on the bed or furniture elevates him to your level, which is not a good idea (the word is "Off!"). Use the "umbilical cord" method, keeping your dog on lead so he has to go with you wherever you go. You sit, he sits. You walk, he heels. You stop, he sit/stays. Everywhere you go, he's with you, but you go first!

when you return and he holds the sit/stay. Increase the distance that you walk away from him before turning until you reach the length of your training leash. But don't rush it! Go back to the beginning if he moves before he should. No matter what the lesson, never be upset by having to back up for a few days. The repetition and practice are what will make your dog reliable in these commands. It won't do any good to move on to something more difficult if the command is not mastered at the easier levels. Above all, even if you do get frustrated, never let your puppy know! Always keep a positive, upbeat attitude during training, which will transmit to your dog for positive results.

The down/stay is taught in the same way once the dog is completely reliable and steady with the down command. Again, don't rush it. With the dog in the down position on your left side, step out on your right foot as you say "Stay." Return by walking around in back of the dog and into your original position. While you are training, it's okay to murmur something like "Hold on" to encourage him to stay put. When the dog will stay without moving when you are at a distance of 3 or 4 feet, begin to increase the length of time before you return. Be sure he holds the down on your return until you say "Okay." At that point, he gets his

MORE PRAISE, LESS FOOD

As you progress with your puppy's lessons, and the puppy is responding well, gradually begin to wean him off the treats by alternating the treats with times when you offer only verbal praise or a few pats on the dog's side. (Pats on the head are dominant actions, so he won't think they are meant to be praise.) Every lesson should end with the puppy's performing the correct action for that session's command. When he gets it right and you withhold the treat, the praise can be as long and lavish as you like. The commands are one word only, but your verbal praise can use as many words as you want...don't skimp!

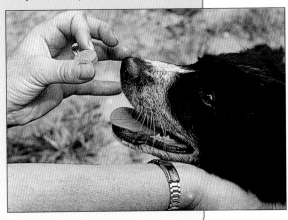

treat—just so he'll remember for next time that it's not over until it's over.

THE COME EXERCISE

No command is more important to the safety of your Border Collie

Practice the come exercise in a variety of settings. Only permit the puppy off lead in a secure area.

so don't overdo it with any of the training. Keep each lesson short. Break it up with a quick run around the yard or a ball toss, repeat the lesson and quit as soon as the pup gets it right. That way, you will always end with a "Good dog."

When the puppy responds to your well-timed "Come," try it with the puppy on the training leash. This time, catch him off guard, while he's sniffing a leaf or watching a bird: "Binky, come!" You may have to pause for a split second after his name to be sure you have his attention. If the puppy shows any sign of confusion, give the leash a mild jerk and take a couple of steps backward. Do not repeat the command. In this case, you should say "Good come" as he reaches you.

than "come." It is what you should say every single time you see the puppy running toward you: "Binky, come! Good dog." During playtime, run a few feet away from the puppy and turn and tell him to "come" as he is already running to you. You can go so far as to teach your puppy two things at once if you squat down and hold out your arms. As the pup gets close to you and you're saying "Good dog," bring your right arm in about waist high. Now he's also learning the hand signal, an excellent device should you be on the phone when you need to get him to come to you! You'll also both be one step ahead when you enter obedience classes.

Puppies, like children, have notoriously short attention spans,

COME AND GET IT!
The come command is your dog's safety signal. Until he is 99% perfect in responding, don't use the come command if you cannot enforce it. Practice on leash with treats or squeakers, or whenever the dog is running to you. Never call him to come to you if he is to be corrected for a misdemeanor. Reward the dog with a treat and happy praise whenever he comes to you.

That's the number-one rule of training. Each command word is given just once. Anything more is nagging. You'll also notice that all commands are one word only. Even when they are actually two words, you say them as one.

Never call the dog to come to you—with or without his name— if you are angry or intend to correct him for some misbehavior. When correcting the pup, you go to him. Your dog must always connect "come" with something pleasant and with your approval; then you can rely on his response.

Life isn't perfect and neither are puppies. A time will come, often around 10 months of age,

when he'll become "selectively deaf" or choose to "forget" his name. He may respond by wagging his tail (and even seeming to smile at you) with a look that says "Make me!" Laugh, throw his favorite toy and skip the lesson you had planned. Pups will be pups!

THE HEEL EXERCISE

The second most important command to teach, after the come, is the heel. When you are walking your growing puppy, you need to be in control. Besides, it looks terrible to be pulled and yanked down the street, and it's not much fun either. Your eight-

Training lessons create a wonderful bond between you and your dog. Thus a well-trained Border Collie is not only a better behaved pet but also a more enjoyable companion.

leash across your chest. Hold the loop and folded leash in your right hand. Pick up the slack leash above the dog in your left hand and hold it loosely at your side. Step out on your left foot as you say "Heel." If the puppy does not move, give a gentle tug or pat your left leg to get him started. If he surges ahead of you, stop and pull him back gently until he is at your side. Tell him to sit and begin again.

Walk a few steps and stop while the puppy is correctly beside you. Tell him to sit and give mild verbal praise. (More enthusiastic praise will encourage him to think the lesson is over.) Repeat the lesson, increasing the number of steps you take only as long as the dog is heeling nicely beside you. When you end the

to ten-week-old puppy will probably follow you everywhere, but that's his natural instinct, not your control over the situation. However, any time he does follow you, you can say "Heel" and be ahead of the game, as he will learn to associate this command with the action of following you before you even begin teaching him to heel.

There is a very precise, almost military, procedure for teaching your dog to heel. As with all other obedience training, begin with the dog on your left side. He will be in a very nice sit and you will have the training

FROM HEEL TO ETERNITY

To begin, step away from the dog, who is in the sit position, on your right foot. That tells the dog you aren't going anywhere. Turn and stand directly in front of him so he won't be tempted to follow. Two seconds is a long, long time to your dog, so increase the time for which he's expected to stay only in short increments. Don't force it. When practicing the heel exercise, your dog will sit at your side whenever you stop. Don't stop for more than three seconds, as your enthusiastic dog will really feel that it's an eternity!

throughout all of his lessons, and now it's time to break the treat habit. Begin by giving him treats at the end of each lesson only. Then start to give a treat after the end of only some of the lessons. At the end of every lesson, as well as during the lessons, be consistent with the praise. Your pup now doesn't know whether he'll get a treat or not, but he should keep performing well just in case! Finally, you will stop giving treat rewards entirely. Save them for something brand-new that you want to teach him. Keep up the praise and you'll always have a "good dog."

OBEDIENCE CLASSES

The advantages of an obedience class are that your dog will have to learn amid the distractions of other people and dogs and that your mistakes will be quickly corrected by the trainer.

Teaching your dog to heel requires that he walk alongside you, at your pace, without pulling or jerking the lead. Show dogs exhibit the heel expertly.

lesson, have him hold the sit, then give him the "Okay" to let him know that this is the end of the lesson. Praise him so that he knows he did a good job.

The cure for excessive pulling (a common problem) is to stop when the dog is no more than 2 or 3 feet ahead of you. Guide him back into position and begin again. With a really determined puller, try switching to a head collar. This will automatically turn the pup's head toward you so you can bring him back easily to the heel position. Give quiet, reassuring praise every time the leash goes slack and he's staying with you.

Staying and heeling can take a lot out of a dog, so provide playtime and free-running exercise to shake off the stress when the lessons are over. You don't want him to associate training with all work and no fun.

TAPERING OFF TIDBITS

Your dog has been watching you—and the hand that treats—

LET'S GO!

Many people use "Let's go" instead of "Heel" when teaching their dogs to behave on lead. It sounds more like fun! When beginning to teach the heel, whatever command you use, always step off on your left foot. That's the one next to the dog, who is on your left side, in case you've forgotten. Keep a loose leash. When the dog pulls ahead, stop, bring him back and begin again. Use treats to guide him around turns.

Teaching your dog along with a qualified instructor and other handlers who may have more dog experience than you is another plus of the class environment. The instructor and other handlers can help you to find the most efficient way of teaching your dog a command or exercise. It's often easier to learn by other people's mistakes than your own. You will also learn all of the requirements for competitive obedience trials, in which you can earn titles and go on to advanced jumping and retrieving exercises, which are fun for many dogs. Obedience classes build the foundation needed for many other canine activities (in which we humans are allowed to participate, too!).

TRAINING FOR OTHER ACTIVITIES

Once your dog has basic obedience under his collar and is 12 months of age, you can enter the world of agility training. Dogs think agility is pure fun, like being turned loose in an amusement park full of obstacles! In addition to agility, there are hunting activities for sporting dogs, lure-coursing events for sighthounds, go-to-ground events

No breed proves more agile, trainable and swift than the Border Collie. This deftly trained Border Collie is weaving his way to the top score at an agility trial.

Playing with a flying disc is an excellent pastime for the Border Collie. It's also an ideal outlet for the owner who does not want to do as much running as his dog.

for terriers, racing for the Nordic sled dogs, herding tests and trials for the shepherd breeds and tracking, which is open to all "nosey" dogs (which would include all dogs!). For those who like to volunteer, there is the wonderful feeling of owning a Therapy Dog and visiting hospices, nursing homes and veterans' homes to bring smiles, comfort and companionship to those who live there.

Around the house, your Border Collie can be taught to do some simple chores. You might teach him to carry a basket of household items or to fetch the morning newspaper. The kids can teach the dog all kinds of tricks, from playing hide-and-seek to balancing a biscuit on his nose. A family dog is what rounds out the family. Everything he does beyond sitting in your lap or gazing lovingly at you represents the bonus of owning a dog.

Herding tests and trials give the Border Collie an opportunity to use its natural herding instincts. These events are great fun for dog, handler and audience alike.

HEALTH PROBLEMS SEEN IN BORDER COLLIES

HIP DYSPLASIA AND ELBOW DYSPLASIA

Hip dysplasia (HD) is manifested by the malformation of the hip joint and its not properly fitting into the socket. Studies indicate that the disease is 70% hereditary and 30% environmental. In Border Collies, the environmental factors include oversupplementation and feeding as well as strenuous play for puppies. Young Border Collies should never be started on work before the age of one year. Compared to some other breeds, the Border Collie suffers from a relatively high incidence of HD, with only over 50% "normal" and about 7% "moderate" to "severe." Incidence of elbow dysplasia remains low; unilateral and bilateral both occur in the breed.

FOCAL/MULTIFOCAL ACQUIRED RETINOPATHY

Focal/Multifocal Acquired Retinopathy (FMAR) causes retinal lesions in Border Collies and other herding dogs as well as in many other performance dogs such as Greyhounds and Siberian Huskies. FMAR may be inherited, but it has not been conclusively determined. It is often confused with PRA or dismissed as scars from distemper or worm infestation. It is more often seen in males and has become alarmingly common in Border Collies.

CEROID LIPOFUSCINOSIS

Ceroid Lipofuscinosis (CL) is an inherited disease that affects the Border Collie. CL is characterized by abnormal behavior, blindness and mental vagueness. Brain atrophy accompanied by high accumulation of ceroid bodies in nerve tissues describes the disease.

HEREDITARY NEUTROPENIA

Hereditary Neutropenia (Trapped Neutrophil Syndrome or TNS) Documented in Border Collies in Australia and New Zealand, TNS, a rare disease suspected to be hereditary, affects puppies between the ages of two weeks and seven months, causing lameness, diarrhea, high temperature and inappetence. Examinations show that puppies have low numbers of neutrophils (a type of white blood cell released from bone marrow), thus causing the pups' inability to fight bacteria and develop properly.

SUPERFICIAL STROMAL KERATITIS

Superficial Stromal Keratitis (SSK), a progressive disease that affects the cornea, known variously as pannus or chronic stromal keratitis, has been documented in the Border Collie, though German Shepherds are most commonly affected. Believed to be caused by exposure to ultraviolet light, SSK results in a film covering the corneal surface. Blindness occurs if left undiagnosed or treated. Use of cortisone under a vet's supervision may prevent onset of blindness, though no cure has been found.

EPILEPSY

Epilepsy is a seizure disorder that has been found in many lines of Border Collies. Since there are no tests for epilepsy and the disorder can occur later in life, it is difficult to breed epilepsy out of a line. Breeders are strongly discouraged from breeding a known epileptic dog.

COLLIE EYE ANOMALY

Collie Eye Anomaly (CEA) affects the correct formation of the eye in herding breeds. In the Border Collie, the disease resembles CEA in Rough and Smooth Collies and is likely inherited as an autosomal recessive trait. In the worst cases, blindness occurs preceded by retinal detachments and hemorrhages.

PROGRESSIVE RETINAL ATROPHY

Progressive Retinal Atrophy (PRA) is a blinding hereditary disorder seen in most pure-bred dogs. Early signs of PRA include nightblindness, inability to adjust vision in dim light and eventual failing day vision. The rods and later the cones are affected, eventually causing blindness. Border Collies most often develop PRA at two years or older.

CENTRAL PROGRESSIVE RETINAL ATROPHY

Central Progressive Retinal Atrophy (CPRA), once widespread in the breed, appears to be disappearing in most Border Collies. The disease is hereditary but seems to be preventable through diet and certain environmental factors. CPRA affects the retinal pigment epithelium, a layer of cells that nourish the retinal nerve cells.

HEALTHCARE OF YOUR

BORDER COLLIE

By Lowell Ackerman DVM, DACVD

HEALTHCARE FOR A LIFETIME

When you own a dog, you become his healthcare advocate over his entire lifespan, as well as being the one to shoulder the financial burden of such care. Accordingly, it is worthwhile to focus on prevention rather than treatment, as you and your pet will both be happier.

Of course, the best place to have begun your program of preventive healthcare is with the initial purchase or adoption of your dog. There is no way of guaranteeing that your new furry friend is free of medical problems, but there are some things you can do to improve your odds. You certainly should have done adequate research into the Border Collie and have selected your puppy carefully rather than buying on impulse. Health issues aside, a large number of pet abandonment and relinquishment cases arise from a mismatch between pet needs and owner expectations. This is entirely preventable with appropriate planning and finding a good breeder.

Regarding healthcare issues specifically, it is very difficult to make blanket statements about where to acquire a problem-free pet, but, again, a reputable breeder is your best bet. In an ideal situation you have the opportunity to see both parents, get references from other owners of the breeder's pups and see genetic-testing documentation for several generations of the litter's ancestors. At the very least, you must thoroughly investigate the

Not only are you your Border Collie's best friend and teacher, you also are his healthcare advocate.

All veterinarians are licensed and all have been taught to read x-rays, but there are specialists called veterinary radiologists who are consulted for the fine details of x-ray interpretations.

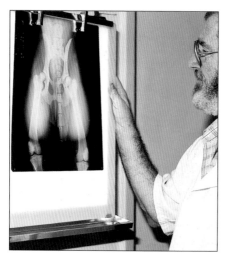

Border Collie and the problems inherent in the breed, as well as the genetic testing available to screen for those problems. Genetic testing offers some important benefits, but testing is available for only a few disorders in a relatively small number of breeds and is not available for some of the most common genetic diseases, such as hip dysplasia, cataracts, epilepsy, cardiomyopathy, etc. This area of research is indeed exciting and increasingly important, and advances will continue to be made each year. In fact, recent research has shown that there is an equivalent dog gene for 75% of known human genes, so research done in either species is likely to benefit the other.

We've also discussed that evaluating the behavioral nature of your Border Collie and that of his immediate family members is an important part of the selection process that cannot be underestimated or overemphasized. It is sometimes difficult to evaluate temperament in puppies because certain behavioral tendencies, such as some forms of aggression, may not be immediately evident. More dogs are euthanized each year for behavioral reasons than for all medical conditions combined, so it is critical to take temperament issues seriously. Start with a well-balanced, friendly companion and put the time and effort into proper socialization, and you will both be rewarded with a lifelong valued relationship.

Assuming that you have started off with a pup from healthy, sound stock, you then become responsible for helping your veterinarian keep your pet healthy. Some crucial things happen before you even bring your puppy home. Parasite control typically begins at two weeks of age, and vaccinations typically begin at six to eight weeks of age. A pre-pubertal evaluation is typically scheduled for about six months of age. At this time, a dental evaluation is done (since the adult teeth are now in), heartworm prevention is started and neutering or spaying is most commonly done.

It is critical to commence regular dental care at home if you have not already done so. It may not sound very important, but most dogs have active periodontal disease by four years of age if they don't have their teeth cleaned regularly at home, not just at their veterinary exams. Dental problems lead to more than just bad "doggie breath": gum disease can have very serious medical consequences. If you start brushing your dog's teeth and using antiseptic rinses from a young age, your dog will be accustomed to it and will not resist. The results will be healthy dentition, which your pet will need to enjoy a long, healthy life.

Most dogs are considered adults at a year of age, although some larger breeds still have some filling out to do up to about two or so years old. Even individual dogs within each breed have different healthcare requirements, so work with your veterinarian to determine what will be needed and what your role should be. This doctor-client relationship is important, because as vaccination guidelines change, there may not be an annual "vaccine visit" scheduled. You must make sure that you see your veterinarian at least annually, even if no vaccines are due, because this is the best opportunity to coordinate health-care activities and to make sure that no medical issues creep by unaddressed.

When your Border Collie reaches three-quarters of his anticipated lifespan, he is considered a

DOGGIE DENTAL DON'TS

A veterinary dental exam is necessary if you notice one or any combination of the following in your dog:
- Broken, loose or missing teeth
- Loss of appetite (which could be due to mouth pain or illness caused by infection)
- Gum abnormalities, including redness, swelling and bleeding
- Drooling, with or without blood
- Yellowing of the teeth or gumline, indicating tartar
- Bad breath

"senior" and likely requires some special care. In general, if you've been taking great care of your canine companion throughout his formative and adult years, the transition to senior status should be a smooth one. Age is not a disease, and as long as everything is functioning as it should, there

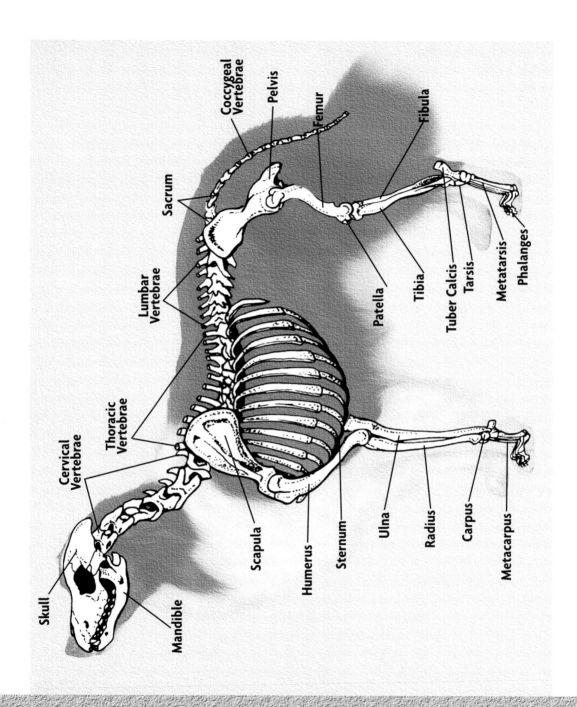

Coccygeal Vertebrae

Pelvis

Femur

Fibula

Sacrum

Lumbar Vertebrae

Patella

Tibia

Tuber Calcis

Tarsis

Metatarsis

Phalanges

Cervical Vertebrae

Thoracic Vertebrae

Scapula

Humerus

Sternum

Ulna

Radius

Carpus

Metacarpus

Skull

Mandible

SKELETAL STRUCTURE OF THE BORDER COLLIE

is no reason why most of late adulthood should not be rewarding for both you and your pet. This is especially true if you have tended to the details, such as regular veterinary visits, proper dental care, excellent nutrition and management of bone and joint issues.

At this stage in your Border Collie's life, your veterinarian may want to schedule visits twice yearly, instead of once, to run some laboratory screenings, electrocardiograms and the like, and to change the diet to something more digestible. Catching problems early is the best way to manage them effectively. Treating the early stages of heart disease is so much easier than trying to intervene when there is more significant damage to the heart muscle. Similarly, managing the beginning of kidney problems is fairly routine if there is no significant kidney damage. Other problems, like cognitive dysfunction (similar to senility and Alzheimer's disease), cancer, diabetes and arthritis, are more common in older dogs, but all can be treated to help the dog live as many happy, comfortable years as possible. Just as in people, medical management is more effective (and less expensive) when you catch things early.

SAMPLE VACCINATION SCHEDULE

6–8 weeks of age	Parvovirus, Distemper, Adenovirus-2 (Hepatitis)
9–11 weeks of age	Parvovirus, Distemper, Adenovirus-2 (Hepatitis)
12–14 weeks of age	Parvovirus, Distemper, Adenovirus-2 (Hepatitis)
16–20 weeks of age	Rabies
1 year of age	Parvovirus, Distemper, Adenovirus-2 (Hepatitis), Rabies

Revaccination is performed every one to three years, depending on the product, the method of administration and the patient's risk. Initial adult inoculation (for dogs at least 16 weeks of age in which a puppy series was not done or could not be confirmed) is two vaccinations, done three to four weeks apart, with revaccination according to the same criteria mentioned. Other vaccines are given as decided between owner and veterinarian.

SELECTING A VETERINARIAN

There is probably no more important decision that you will make regarding your pet's healthcare than the selection of his doctor. Your pet's veterinarian will be a pediatrician, family-practice physician and gerontologist, depending on the dog's life stage, and will be the individual who makes recommendations regarding issues such as when specialists need to be consulted, when diagnostic testing and/or therapeutic intervention is needed and when you will need to seek outside emergency and critical-care services. Your vet will act as your advocate and liaison throughout these processes.

Everyone has his own idea about what to look for in a vet, an individual who will play a big role in his dog's (and, of course, his own) life for many years to come. For some, it is the compassionate caregiver with whom they hope to develop a professional relationship to span the lifetime of their dogs and even their future pets. For others, they are seeking a clinician with keen diagnostic and therapeutic insight who can deliver state-of-the-art healthcare.

Your veterinarian will take your puppy's temperature. Normal temperature for a dog is 100.5 to 102.5° F.

Do You Know About Hip Dysplasia?

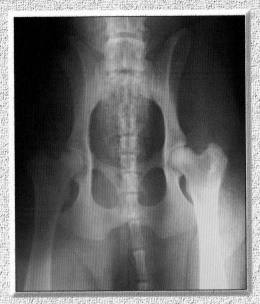

X-ray of a dog with "Good" hips.

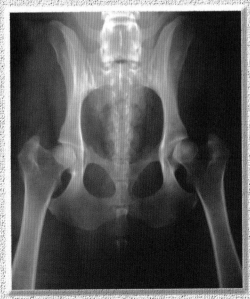

X-ray of a dog with "Moderate" dysplastic hips.

Hip dysplasia is a fairly common condition found in pure-bred dogs. When a dog has hip dysplasia, his hind leg has an incorrectly formed hip joint. By constant use of the hip joint, it becomes more and more loose, wears abnormally and may become arthritic.

Hip dysplasia can only be confirmed with an x-ray, but certain symptoms may indicate a problem. Your dog may have a hip dysplasia problem if he walks in a peculiar manner, hops instead of smoothly runs, uses his hind legs in unison (to keep the pressure off the weak joint), has trouble getting up from a prone position or always sits with both legs together on one side of his body.

As the dog matures, he may adapt well to life with a bad hip, but in a few years the arthritis develops and many dogs with hip dysplasia become crippled.

Hip dysplasia is considered an inherited disease and only can be diagnosed definitively by x-ray when the dog is two years old, although symptoms often appear earlier. Some experts claim that a special diet might help your puppy outgrow the bad hip, but the usual treatments are surgical. The removal of the pectineus muscle, the removal of the round part of the femur, reconstructing the pelvis and replacing the hip with an artificial one are all surgical interventions that are expensive, but they are usually very successful. Follow the advice of your veterinarian.

Common Infectious Diseases

Let's discuss some of the diseases that create the need for vaccination in the first place. Following are the major canine infectious diseases and a simple explanation of each.

Rabies: A devastating viral disease that can be fatal in dogs and people. In fact, vaccination of dogs and cats is an important public-health measure to create a resistant animal buffer population to protect people from contracting the disease. Vaccination schedules are determined on a government level and are not optional for pet owners; rabies vaccination is required by law in all 50 states.

Parvovirus: A severe, potentially life-threatening disease that is easily transmitted between dogs. There are four strains of the virus, but it is believed that there is significant "cross-protection" between strains that may be included in individual vaccines.

Distemper: A potentially severe and life-threatening disease with a relatively high risk of exposure, especially in certain regions. In very high-risk distemper environments, young pups may be vaccinated with human measles vaccine, a related virus that offers cross-protection when administered at four to ten weeks of age.

Hepatitis: Caused by canine adenovirus type 1 (CAV-1), but since vaccination with the causative virus has a higher rate of adverse effects, cross-protection is derived from the use of adenovirus type 2 (CAV-2), a cause of respiratory disease and one of the potential causes of canine cough. Vaccination with CAV-2 provides long-term immunity against hepatitis, but relatively less protection against respiratory infection.

Canine cough: Also called tracheobronchitis, actually a fairly complicated result of viral and bacterial offenders; therefore, even with vaccination, protection is incomplete. Wherever dogs congregate, canine cough will likely be spread among them. Intranasal vaccination with *Bordetella* and parainfluenza is the best safeguard, but the duration of immunity does not appear to be very long, typically a year at most. These are non-core vaccines, but vaccination is sometimes mandated by boarding kennels, obedience classes, dog shows and other places where dogs congregate to try to minimize spread of infection.

Leptospirosis: A potentially fatal disease that is more common in some geographic regions. It is capable of being spread to humans. The disease varies with the individual "serovar," or strain, of *Leptospira* involved. Since there does not appear to be much cross-protection between serovars, protection is only as good as the likelihood that the serovar in the vaccine is the same as the one in the pet's local environment. Problems with *Leptospira* vaccines are that protection does not last very long, side effects are not uncommon and a large percentage of dogs (perhaps 30%) may not respond to vaccination.

Borrelia burgdorferi: The cause of Lyme disease, the risk of which varies with the geographic area in which the pet lives and travels. Lyme disease is spread by deer ticks in the eastern US and western black-legged ticks in the western part of the country, and the risk of exposure is high in some regions. Lameness, fever and inappetence are most commonly seen in affected dogs. The extent of protection from the vaccine has not been conclusively demonstrated.

Coronavirus: This disease has a high risk of exposure, especially in areas where dogs congregate, but it typically causes only mild to moderate digestive upset (diarrhea, vomiting, etc.). Vaccines are available, but the duration of protection is believed to be relatively short and the effectiveness of the vaccine in preventing infection is considered low.

There are many other vaccinations available, including those for *Giardia* and canine adenovirus-1. While there may be some specific indications for their use, and local risk factors to be considered, they are not widely recommended for most dogs.

Still others need a veterinary facility that is open evenings and weekends, or is in close proximity or provides mobile veterinary services, to accommodate their schedules; these people may not much mind that their dogs might see different veterinarians on each visit. Just as we have different reasons for selecting our own healthcare professionals (e.g., covered by insurance plan, expert in field, convenient location, etc.), we should not expect that there is a one-size-fits-all recommendation for selecting a veterinarian and veterinary practice. The best advice is to be honest in your assessment of what you expect from a veterinary practice and to conscientiously research the options in your area. You will quickly appreciate that not all veterinary practices are the same, and you will be happiest with one that truly meets your needs.

There is another point to be considered in the selection of veterinary services. Not that long ago, a single veterinarian would attempt to manage all medical and surgical issues as they arose. That was often problematic, because veterinarians are trained in many species and many diseases, and it was just impossible for general veterinary practitioners to be experts in every species, every field and every ailment. However, just as in the human healthcare fields, specialization has allowed general practitioners to concentrate on primary healthcare delivery, especially wellness and the prevention of infectious diseases, and to utilize a network of specialists to assist in the management of conditions that require specific expertise and experience. Thus there are now many types of veterinary specialists, including dermatologists, cardiologists, ophthalmologists, surgeons, internists, oncologists, neurologists, behaviorists, criticalists and others to help primary-care veterinarians deal with complicated medical challenges. In most cases, specialists see cases referred by primary-care veterinarians, make diagnoses and set up management plans. From there, the animals' ongoing care is returned to their primary-care veterinarians. This important team approach to your pet's medical-care needs has provided opportunities for advanced care and an unparalleled level of quality to be delivered.

With all of the opportunities for your Border Collie to receive high-quality veterinary medical care, there is another topic that needs to be addressed at the same time—cost. It's been said that you can have excellent healthcare or inexpensive healthcare, but never both; this is as true in veterinary medicine as it is in human medicine. While veterinary costs are a fraction of what the same services

YOUR DOG NEEDS TO VISIT THE VET IF:

- He has ingested a toxin such as antifreeze or a toxic plant; in these cases, administer first aid and call the vet right away
- His teeth are discolored, loose or missing or he has sores or other signs of infection or abnormality in the mouth
- He has been vomiting, has had diarrhea or has been constipated for over 24 hours; call immediately if you notice blood
- He has refused food for over 24 hours
- His eating habits, water intake or toilet habits have noticeably changed; if you have noticed weight gain or weight loss
- He shows symptoms of bloat, which requires immediate attention
- He is salivating excessively
- He has a lump in his throat
- He has a lumps or bumps anywhere on the body
- He is very lethargic
- He appears to be in pain or otherwise has trouble chewing or swallowing
- His skin loses elasticity.

Of course, there will be other instances in which a visit to the vet is necessary; these are just some of the signs that could be indicative of serious problems that need to be caught as early as possible.

cost in the human healthcare arena, it is still difficult to deal with unanticipated medical costs, especially since they can easily creep into hundreds or even thousands of dollars if specialists or emergency services become involved. However, there are ways of managing these risks. The easiest is to buy pet health insurance and realize that its foremost purpose is not to cover routine healthcare visits but rather to serve as an umbrella for those rainy days when your pet needs medical care and you don't want to worry about whether or not you can afford that care.

Pet insurance policies are very cost-effective (and very inexpensive by human health-insurance standards), but make sure that you buy the policy long before you intend to use it (preferably starting in puppyhood, because coverage will exclude pre-existing conditions) and that you are actually buying an indemnity insurance plan from an insurance company that is regulated by your state or province. Many insurance policy look-alikes are actually discount clubs that are redeemable only at specific locations and for specific services. An indemnity plan covers your pet at almost all veterinary, specialty and emergency practices and is an excellent way to manage your pet's ongoing healthcare needs.

VACCINATIONS AND INFECTIOUS DISEASES

There has never been an easier time to prevent a variety of infectious diseases in your dog, but the advances we've made in veterinary medicine come with a price—choice. Now while it may seem that choice is a good thing (and it is), it has never been more difficult for the pet owner (or the veterinarian) to make an informed decision about the best way to protect pets through vaccination.

Years ago, it was just accepted that puppies got a starter series of vaccinations and then annual "boosters" throughout their lives to keep them protected. As more and more vaccines became available, consumers wanted the convenience of having all of that protection in a single injection. The result was "multivalent" vaccines that crammed a lot of protection into a single syringe. The manufacturers' recommendations were to give the vaccines annually, and this was a simple enough protocol to follow. However, as veterinary medicine has become more sophisticated and we have started looking more at healthcare quandaries rather than convenience, it became necessary to reevaluate the situation and deal with some tough questions. It is important to realize that whether or not to use a particular vaccine depends on the risk of contracting the disease against which it protects, the severity of the disease if it is contracted, the duration of immunity provided by the vaccine, the safety of the product and the needs of the individual animal. In a very general sense, rabies, distemper, hepatitis and parvovirus are considered core vaccine needs, while parainfluenza, *Bordetella bronchiseptica*, leptospirosis, coronavirus

and borreliosis (Lyme disease) are considered non-core needs and best reserved for animals that demonstrate reasonable risk of contracting the diseases.

Border Collies pick up fleas and ticks because they spend so much time in grass where these parasites hide awaiting a suitable host.

NEUTERING/SPAYING

Sterilization procedures (neutering for males/spaying for females) are meant to accomplish several purposes. While the underlying premise is to address the risk of pet overpopulation, there are also some medical and behavioral benefits to the surgeries as well. For females, spaying prior to the first estrus (heat cycle) leads to a marked reduction in the risk of mammary cancer. There also will be no manifestations of "heat" to attract male dogs and no bleeding in the house. For males, there is prevention of testicular cancer and a reduction in the risk of prostate problems. In both sexes there may be some limited reduction in aggressive behaviors toward other dogs, and some diminishing of urine marking, roaming and mounting.

While neutering and spaying do indeed prevent animals from contributing to pet overpopulation, even no-cost and low-cost neutering options have not eliminated the problem. Perhaps one of the main reasons for this is that individuals who intentionally breed their dogs and those who allow their animals to run at large are the main causes of unwanted offspring. Also, animals in shelters are often there because they were abandoned or relinquished, not because they came from unplanned matings. Neutering/spaying is important, but it should be considered in the context of the real causes of animals' ending up in shelters and eventually being euthanized.

One of the important considerations regarding neutering is

SPAY'S THE WAY

Although spaying a female dog qualifies as major surgery—an ovariohysterectomy, in fact—this procedure is regarded as routine when performed by a qualified veterinarian on a healthy dog. The advantages to spaying a bitch are many and great. Spayed dogs do not develop uterine cancer or any life-threatening diseases of the genitals. Likewise, spayed dogs are at a significantly reduced risk of breast cancer. Bitches (and owners) are relieved of the demands of heat cycles. A spayed bitch will not leave bloody stains on your furniture during estrus, and you will not have to contend with single-minded macho males trying to climb your fence in order to seduce her. The spayed bitch's coat will not show the ill effects of her estrogen level's climbing such as a dull, lackluster outer coat or patches of hairlessness.

that it is a surgical procedure. This sometimes gets lost in discussions of low-cost procedures and commoditization of the process. In females, spaying is specifically referred to as an ovariohysterectomy. In this procedure, a midline incision is made in the abdomen and the entire uterus and both ovaries are surgically removed. While this is a major invasive surgical procedure, it usually has few complications, because it is typically performed on healthy young animals. However, it is major surgery, as any woman who has had a hysterectomy will attest.

In males, neutering has traditionally referred to castration, which involves the surgical removal of both testicles. While still a significant piece of surgery, there is not the abdominal exposure that is required in the female surgery. In addition, there is now a chemical sterilization option, in which a solution is injected into each testicle, leading to atrophy of the sperm-producing cells. This can typically be done under sedation rather than full anesthesia. This is a relatively new approach, and there are no long-term clinical studies yet available.

Neutering/spaying is typically done around six months of age at most veterinary hospitals, although techniques have been pioneered to perform the procedures in animals as young as eight weeks of age. In general, the surgeries on the very young animals are done for the specific reason of sterilizing them before they go to their new homes. This is done in some shelter hospitals for assurance that the animals will definitely not produce any pups. Otherwise, these organizations need to rely on owners to comply with their wishes to have the animals "altered" at a later date, something that does not always happen.

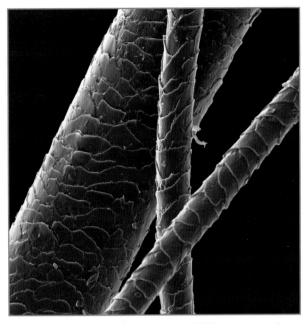

The photo above show normal dog hair magnified 60-150 times its actual size. The photo below show distressed hair that is frayed.

S. E. M. by Dr. Dennis Kunkel, University of Hawaii

A scanning electron micrograph of a dog flea, *Ctenocephalides canis*, on dog hair.

EXTERNAL PARASITES

FLEAS

Fleas have been around for millions of years and, while we have better tools now for controlling them than at any time in the past, there still is little chance that they will end up on an endangered species list. Actually, they are very well adapted to living on our pets, and they continue to adapt as we make advances.

The female flea can consume 15 times her weight in blood during active reproduction and can lay as many as 40 eggs a day. These eggs are very resistant to the effects of insecticides. They hatch into larvae, which then mature and spin cocoons. The immature fleas reside in this pupal stage until the time is right for feeding. This pupal stage is also very resistant to the effects of insecticides, and pupae can last in the environment without feeding for many months. Newly emergent fleas are attracted to animals by the warmth of the animals' bodies, movement and exhaled carbon dioxide. However, when they first emerge from their cocoons, they orient towards light; thus when an animal passes between a flea and the light source, casting a shadow, the flea pounces and starts to feed. If the animal turns out to be a dog or cat, the reproductive cycle continues. If the flea lands on another type of animal, including a person, the flea will bite but will then look for a more appropriate host. An emerging adult flea can survive without feeding for up to 12 months but, once it tastes blood, it can survive off its host for only three to four days.

It was once thought that fleas spend most of their lives in the environment, but we now know that fleas won't willingly jump off a dog unless leaping to another dog or when physically removed by brushing, bathing or other manipulation. Flea eggs, on the other hand, are shiny and smooth, and they roll off the animal and into the environment. The eggs, larvae and pupae then exist in the environment, but once the adult finds a susceptible animal, it's home sweet home until the flea is forced to seek refuge elsewhere.

Since adult fleas live on the animal and immature forms survive in the environment, a successful treatment plan must address all stages of the flea life cycle. There are now several safe and effective flea-control products that can be applied on a monthly

FLEA PREVENTION FOR YOUR DOG
- Discuss with your veterinarian the safest product to protect your dog, likely in the form of a monthly tablet or a liquid preparation placed on the back of the dog's neck.
- For dogs suffering from flea-bite dermatitis, a shampoo or topical insecticide treatment is required.
- Your lawn and property should be sprayed with an insecticide designed to kill fleas and ticks that lurk outdoors.
- Using a flea comb, check the dog's coat regularly for any signs of parasites.
- Practice good housekeeping. Vacuum floors, carpets and furniture regularly, especially in the areas that the dog frequents, and wash the dog's bedding weekly.
- Follow up house-cleaning with carpet shampoos and sprays to rid the house of fleas at all stages of development. Insect growth regulators are the safest option.

basis. These include fipronil, imidacloprid, selamectin and permethrin (found in several formulations). Most of these products have significant flea-killing rates within 24 hours. However, none of them will control the immature forms in the environment. To accomplish this, there are a variety of insect growth regulators that can be sprayed into

THE FLEA'S LIFE CYCLE

What came first, the flea or the egg? This age-old mystery is more difficult to comprehend than the

actual cycle of the flea. Fleas usually live only about four months. A female can lay 2,000 eggs in her lifetime.

Egg

After ten days of rolling around your carpet or under your furniture, the eggs hatch into larvae, which feed on various and sundry debris. In days or

Larva

months, depending on the climate, the larvae spin cocoons and develop into the pupal or nymph stage, which quickly develop into fleas.

Pupa

These immature fleas must locate a host within 10 to 14 days or they will die. Only about 1% of the flea population exist as adult fleas, while the other 99% exist as eggs, larvae or pupae.

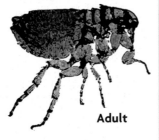

Adult

KILL FLEAS THE NATURAL WAY

If you choose not to go the route of conventional medication, there are some natural ways to ward off fleas:

- Dust your dog with a natural flea powder, composed of such herbal goodies as rosemary, wormwood, pennyroyal, citronella, rue, tobacco powder and eucalyptus.
- Apply diatomaceous earth, the fossilized remains of single-cell algae, to your carpets, furniture and pet's bedding. Even though it's not good for dogs, it's even worse for fleas, which will dry up swiftly and die.
- Brush your dog frequently, give him adequate exercise and let him fast occasionally. All of these activities strengthen the dog's system and make him more resistant to disease and parasites.
- Bathe your dog with a capful of pennyroyal or eucalyptus oil.
- Feed a natural diet, free of additives and preservatives. Add some fresh garlic and brewer's yeast to the dog's morning portion, as these items have flea-repelling properties.

the environment (e.g., pyriprox-yfen, methoprene, fenoxycarb) as well as insect development inhibitors such as lufenuron that can be administered. These compounds have no effect on adult fleas, but they stop imma-ture forms from developing into

adults. In years gone by we relied heavily on toxic insecticides (such as organophosphates, organochlo-rines and carbamates) to manage the flea problem, but today's options are not only much safer to use on our pets but also safer for the environment.

TICKS

Ticks are members of the spider class (arachnids) and are blood-sucking parasites capable of transmitting a variety of diseases, including Lyme disease, ehrlichiosis, babesiosis and Rocky Mountain spotted fever. It's easy to see ticks on your own skin, but it is more of a challenge when your dog is affected. Whenever you happen to be planning a stroll in a tick-infested area (especially forests, grassy or wooded areas or parks) be prepared to do a thorough inspection of your dog afterward to search for ticks. Ticks can be tricky, so make sure you spend time looking in the ears, between the toes and everywhere else where a tick might hide. Ticks need to be attached for 24–72 hours before they transmit most of the diseases that they carry, so you do have a window of opportunity for some preventive intervention.

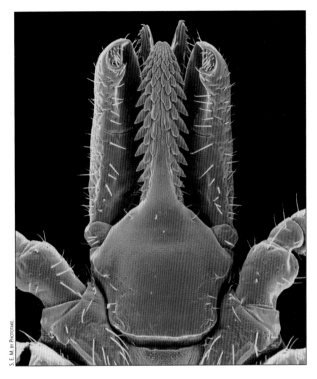

S. E. M. BY PHOTOTAKE

A TICKING BOMB

There is nothing good about a tick's harpooning his nose into your dog's skin. Among the diseases caused by ticks are Rocky Mountain spotted fever, canine ehrlichiosis, canine babesiosis, canine hepatozoonosis and Lyme disease. If a dog is allergic to the saliva of a female wood tick, he can develop tick paralysis.

Female ticks live to eat and breed. They can lay between 4,000 and 5,000 eggs and they die soon after. Males, on the other hand, live only to mate with the females and continue the process as long as they are able. Most ticks live on multiple hosts before parasitizing dogs. The immature forms typically reside on grass and shrubs, waiting for susceptible animals to walk by. The larvae and nymph stages typically feed on wildlife.

If only a few ticks are present on a dog, they can be plucked out, but it is important to remove the entire head and mouthparts,

A scanning electron micrograph of the head of a female deer tick, *Ixodes dammini*, a parasitic tick that carries Lyme disease.

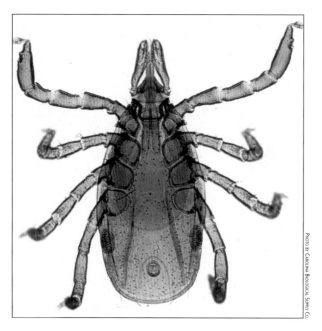

PHOTO BY CAROLINA BIOLOGICAL SUPPLY CO.

Deer tick, *Ixodes dammini.*

of in a container of alcohol or household bleach.

Some of the newer flea products, specifically those with fipronil, selamectin and permethrin, have effect against some, but not all, species of tick. Flea collars containing appropriate pesticides (e.g., propoxur, chlorfenvinphos) can aid in tick control. In most areas, such collars should be placed on animals in March, at the beginning of the tick season, and changed regularly. Leaving the collar on when the pesticide level is waning invites the development of resistance. Amitraz collars are also good for tick control, and the active ingredient does not interfere with other flea-control products. The ingredient helps prevent the attachment of ticks to the skin and will cause those ticks already on the skin to detach themselves.

which may be deeply embedded in the skin. This is best accomplished with forceps designed especially for this purpose; fingers can be used but should be protected with rubber gloves, plastic wrap or at least a paper towel. The tick should be grasped as closely as possible to the animal's skin and should be pulled upward with steady, even pressure. Do not squeeze, crush or puncture the body of the tick or you risk exposure to any disease carried by that tick. Once the ticks have been removed, the sites of attachment should be disinfected. Your hands should then be washed with soap and water to further minimize risk of contagion. The tick should be disposed

TICK CONTROL
Removal of underbrush and leaf litter and the thinning of trees in areas where tick control is desired are recommended. These actions remove the cover and food sources for small animals that serve as hosts for ticks. With continued mowing of grasses in these areas, the probability of ticks' surviving is further reduced. A variety of insecticide ingredients (e.g., resmethrin, carbaryl, permethrin, chlorpyrifos, dioxathion and allethrin) are registered for tick control around the home.

MITES

Mites are tiny arachnid parasites that parasitize the skin of dogs. Skin diseases caused by mites are referred to as "mange," and there are many different forms seen in dogs. These forms are very different from one another, each one warranting an individual description.

Sarcoptic mange, or scabies, is one of the itchiest conditions that affects dogs. The microscopic *Sarcoptes* mites burrow into the superficial layers of the skin and can drive dogs crazy with itchiness. They are also communicable to people, although they can't complete their reproductive cycle on people. In addition to being tiny, the mites also are often difficult to find when trying to make a diagnosis. Skin scrapings from multiple areas are examined microscopically but, even then, sometimes the mites cannot be found.

Fortunately, scabies is relatively easy to treat, and there are a variety of products that will successfully kill the mites. Since the mites can't live in the environment for very long without feeding, a complete cure is usually possible within four to eight weeks.

Cheyletiellosis is caused by a relatively large mite, which sometimes can be seen even without a microscope. Often referred to as "walking dandruff," this also causes itching, but not usually as profound as with

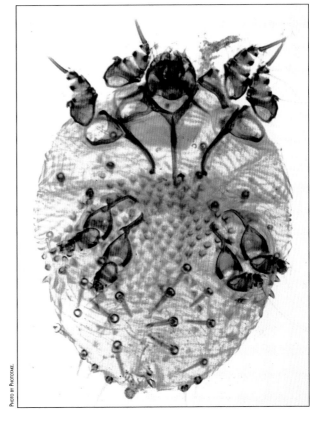

PHOTO BY PHOTOTAKE.

Sarcoptes scabiei, commonly known as the "itch mite."

scabies. While *Cheyletiella* mites can survive somewhat longer in the environment than scabies mites, they too are relatively easy to treat, being responsive to not only the medications used to treat scabies but also often to flea-control products.

Otodectes cynotis is the canine ear mite and is one of the more common causes of mange, especially in young dogs in shelters or pet stores. That's because the mites are typically present in large numbers and are quickly spread to

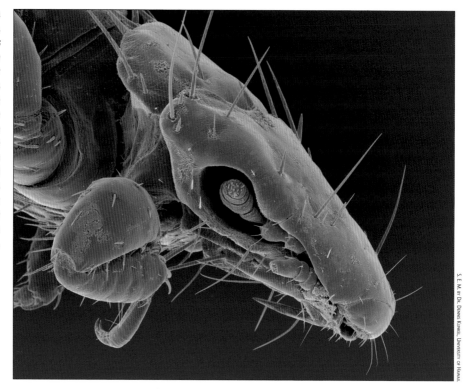

Micrograph of a dog louse, *Heterodoxus spiniger*. Female lice attach their eggs to the hairs of the dog. As the eggs hatch, the larval lice bite and feed on the blood. Lice can also feed on dead skin and hair. This feeding activity can cause hair loss and skin problems.

S. E. M. by Dr. Dennis Kunkel, University of Hawaii

nearby animals. The mites rarely do much harm but can be difficult to eradicate if the treatment regimen is not comprehensive. While many try to treat the condition with ear drops only, this is the most common cause of treatment failure. Ear drops cause the mites to simply move out of the ears and as far away as possible (usually to the base of the tail) until the insecticide levels in the ears drop to an acceptable level—then it's back to business as usual! The successful treatment of ear mites requires treating all animals in the household with a systemic insecticide, such as selamectin, or a combi-

nation of miticidal ear drops combined with whole-body flea-control preparations.

Demodicosis, sometimes referred to as red mange, can be one of the most difficult forms of mange to treat. Part of the problem has to do with the fact that the mites live in the hair follicles and they are relatively well shielded from topical and systemic products. The main issue, however, is that demodectic mange typically results only when there is some underlying process interfering with the dog's immune system.

Since *Demodex* mites are

normal residents of the skin of mammals, including humans, there is usually a mite population explosion only when the immune system fails to keep the number of mites in check. In young animals, the immune deficit may be transient or may reflect an actual inherited immune problem. In older animals, demodicosis is usually seen only when there is another disease hampering the immune system, such as diabetes, cancer, thyroid problems or the use of immune-suppressing drugs. Accordingly, treatment involves not only trying to kill the mange mites but also discerning what is interfering with immune function and correcting it if possible.

Chiggers represent several different species of mite that don't parasitize dogs specifically, but do latch on to passersby and can cause irritation. The problem is most prevalent in wooded areas in the late summer and fall. Treatment is not difficult, as the mites do not complete their life cycle on dogs and are susceptible to a variety of miticidal products.

MOSQUITOES

Mosquitoes have long been known to transmit a variety of diseases to people, as well as just being biting pests during warm weather. They also pose a real risk to pets. Not only do they carry deadly heartworms but recently there also has been much concern over their involvement with West Nile virus. While we can avoid heartworm with the use of preventive medications, there are no such preventives for West Nile virus. The only method of prevention in endemic areas is active mosquito control. Fortunately, most dogs that have been exposed to the virus only developed flu-like symptoms and, to date, there have not been the large number of reported deaths in canines as seen in some other species.

Illustration of *Demodex folliculoram.*

MOSQUITO REPELLENT

Low concentrations of DEET (less than 10%), found in many human mosquito repellents, have been safely used in dogs but, in these concentrations, probably give only about two hours of protection. DEET may be safe in these small concentrations, but since it is not licensed for use on dogs, there is no research proving its safety for dogs. Products containing permethrin give the longest-lasting protection, perhaps two to four weeks. As DEET is not licensed for use on dogs, and both DEET and permethrin can be quite toxic to cats, appropriate care should be exercised. Other products, such as those containing oil of citronella, also have some mosquito-repellent activity, but typically have a relatively short duration of action.

S. E. M. by Dr. Dennis Kunkel, University of Hawaii; Inset by Tam C. Nguyen

The ascarid roundworm *Toxocara canis*, showing the mouth with three lips. INSET: Photomicrograph of the roundworm *Ascaris lumbricoides*.

INTERNAL PARASITES: WORMS

ASCARIDS

Ascarids are intestinal roundworms that rarely cause severe disease in dogs. Nonetheless, they are of major public health significance because they can be transferred to people. Sadly, it is children who are most commonly affected by the parasite, probably from inadvertently ingesting ascarid-contaminated soil. In fact, many yards and children's sandboxes contain appreciable numbers of ascarid eggs. So, while ascarids don't bite dogs or latch onto their intestines to suck blood, they do cause some nasty medical conditions in children and are best eradicated from our furry friends. Because pups can start passing ascarid eggs by three weeks of age, most parasite-control programs begin at two weeks of age and are repeated every two weeks until pups are eight weeks old. It is important to

S. E. M. BY DR. DENNIS KUNKEL, UNIVERSITY OF HAWAII.

realize that bitches can pass ascarids to their pups even if they test negative prior to whelping. Accordingly, bitches are best treated at the same time as the pups.

HOOKWORMS

Unlike ascarids, hookworms do latch onto a dog's intestinal tract and can cause significant loss of blood and protein. Similar to ascarids, hookworms can be transmitted to humans, where they cause a condition known as cutaneous larval migrans. Dogs can become infected either by consuming the infective larvae or by the larvae's penetrating the skin directly. People most often get infected when they are lying on the ground (such as on a beach) and the larvae penetrate the skin. Yes, the larvae can penetrate through a beach blanket. Hookworms are typically susceptible to the same medications used to treat ascarids.

The hookworm *Ancylostoma caninum* infests the colon of dogs. INSET: Note the row of hooks at the posterior end, used to anchor the worm to the intestinal wall.

WHIPWORMS

Whipworms latch onto the lower aspects of the dog's colon and can cause cramping and diarrhea. Eggs do not start to appear in the dog's feces until about three months after the dog was infected. This worm has a peculiar life cycle, which makes it more difficult to control than ascarids or hookworms. The good thing is that whipworms rarely are transferred to people.

Some of the medications used to treat ascarids and hookworms are also effective against whipworms, but, in general, a separate treatment protocol is needed. Since most of the medications are effective against the adults but not the eggs or larvae, treatment is typically repeated in three weeks, and then often in three

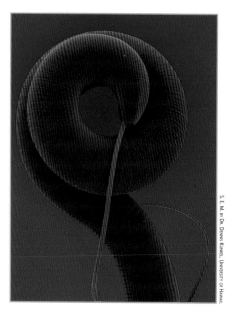

Adult whipworm, *Trichuris* sp., an intestinal parasite.

S. E. M. BY DR. DENNIS KUNKEL, UNIVERSITY OF HAWAII.

WORM-CONTROL GUIDELINES

- Practice sanitary habits with your dog and home.
- Clean up after your dog and don't let him sniff or eat other dogs' droppings.
- Control insects and fleas in the dog's environment. Fleas, lice, cockroaches, beetles, mice and rats can act as hosts for various worms.
- Prevent dogs from eating uncooked meat, raw poultry and dead animals.
- Keep dogs and children from playing in sand and soil.
- Kennel dogs on cement or gravel; avoid dirt runs.
- Administer heartworm preventives regularly.
- Have your vet examine your dog's stools at your annual visits.
- Select a boarding kennel carefully so as to avoid contamination from other dogs or an unsanitary environment.
- Prevent dogs from roaming. Obey local leash laws.

months as well. Unfortunately, since dogs don't develop resistance to whipworms, it is difficult to prevent them from getting reinfected if they visit soil contaminated with whipworm eggs.

TAPEWORMS

There are many different species of tapeworm that affect dogs, but *Dipylidium caninum* is probably the most common and is spread by fleas. Flea larvae feed on organic debris and tapeworm eggs in the environment and, when a dog chews at himself and manages to ingest fleas, he might get a dose of tapeworm at the same time. The tapeworm then develops further in the intestine of the dog.

The tapeworm itself, which latches onto the intestinal wall, is composed of numerous segments. When the segments break off into the intestine (as proglottids), they may accumulate around the rectum, like grains of rice. While this tapeworm is disgusting in its behavior, it is not directly communicable to humans (although humans can also get infected by swallowing fleas).

A much more dangerous flatworm is *Echinococcus multilocularis*, which is typically found in foxes, coyotes and wolves. The eggs are passed in the feces and infect rodents, and, when dogs eat the rodents, the dogs can be infected by thousands of adult tapeworms. While the parasites don't cause many problems in dogs, this is considered the most lethal worm infection that people can get. Take appropriate precautions if you live in an area in which these tapeworms are found. Do not use mulch that may contain feces of dogs, cats or wildlife, and discourage your pets from hunting

wildlife. Treat these tapeworm infections aggressively in pets, because if humans get infected, approximately half die.

HEARTWORMS

Heartworm disease is caused by the parasite *Dirofilaria immitis* and is seen in dogs around the world. A member of the roundworm group, it is spread between dogs by the bite of an infected mosquito. The mosquito injects infective larvae into the dog's skin with its bite, and these larvae develop under the skin for a period of time before making their way to the heart. There they develop into adults, which grow and create blockages of the heart, lungs and major blood vessels there. They also start producing offspring (microfilariae)

A dog tapeworm proglottid (body segment).

The dog tapeworm *Taenia pisiformis*.

S. E. M. BY DR. DENNIS KUNKEL, UNIVERSITY OF HAWAII.

A Look at Internal Parasites

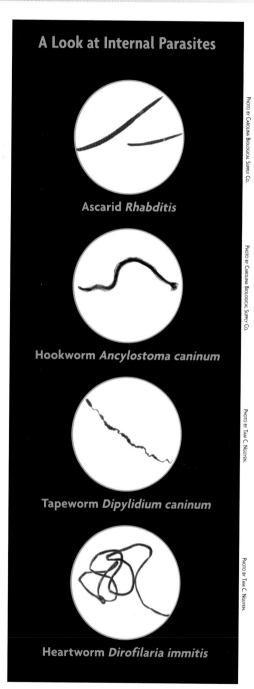

Ascarid *Rhabditis*

Hookworm *Ancylostoma caninum*

Tapeworm *Dipylidium caninum*

Heartworm *Dirofilaria immitis*

and these microfilariae circulate in the bloodstream, waiting to hitch a ride when the next mosquito bites. Once in the mosquito, the microfilariae develop into infective larvae and the entire process is repeated.

When dogs get infected with heartworm, over time they tend to develop symptoms associated with heart disease, such as coughing, exercise intolerance and potentially many other manifestations. Diagnosis is confirmed by either seeing the microfilariae themselves in blood samples or using immunologic tests (antigen testing) to identify the presence of adult heartworms. Since antigen tests measure the presence of adult heartworms and microfilarial tests measure offspring produced by adults, neither are positive until six to seven months after the initial infection. However, the beginning of damage can occur by fifth-stage larvae as early as three months after infection. Thus it is possible for dogs to be harboring problem-causing larvae for up to three months before either type of test would identify an infection.

The good news is that there are great protocols available for preventing heartworm in dogs. Discuss with your veterinarian the best course of action with your Border Collie. Keep in mind that ivermectin, the most common oral preventive drug, has been found harmful in collie breeds.

BORDER COLLIE

When we bring home a puppy, full of the energy and exuberance that accompanies youth, we hope for a long, happy and fulfilling relationship with the new family member. Even when we adopt an older dog, we look forward to the years of companionship ahead with a new canine friend. However, aging is inevitable for all creatures, and there will come a time when your Border Collie reaches his senior years and will need special considerations and attention to his care.

WHEN IS MY DOG A "SENIOR"?

In general, purebred dogs are considered to have achieved senior status when they reach 75% of their breed's average lifespan, with lifespan being based on breed size. Your Border Collie has an average lifespan of 14 years and thus is a senior citizen at around 10 years of age.

Obviously, the old "seven dog years to one human year" theory is not exact. In puppyhood, a dog's year is actually comparable to more than seven human years, considering the puppy's rapid growth during his first year. Then, in adulthood, the ratio decreases.

Regardless, the more viable rule of thumb is that the larger the dog, the shorter his expected lifespan. Of course, this can vary among individual dogs, with many living longer than expected, which we hope is the case!

The Border Collie enjoys a lifespan of about 14 years, which is an impressive life expectancy for any dog.

WHAT ARE THE SIGNS OF AGING?

By the time your dog has reached his senior years, you will know him very well, so the physical and behavioral changes that accompany aging should be noticeable to you. Humans and dogs share the most obvious physical sign of aging: gray hair! Graying often occurs first on the muzzle and face, around the eyes. Other telltale signs are the dog's overall decrease in activity. Your

When your dog refuses to climb the stairs that he has climbed for years, you will know that he is "not the dog he used to be." Treat seniors with extra care.

older dog might be more content to nap and rest, and he may not show the same old enthusiasm when it's time to play in the yard or go for a walk. Other physical signs include significant weight loss or gain; more labored movement; skin and coat problems, possibly hair loss; sight and/or hearing problems; changes in toileting habits, perhaps seeming "unhousebroken" at times; tooth decay, bad breath or other mouth problems.

There are behavioral changes that go along with aging, too. There are numerous causes for behavioral changes. Sometimes a

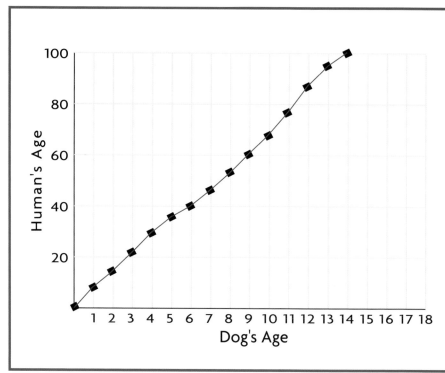

dog's apparent confusion results from a physical change like diminished sight or hearing. If his confusion causes him to be afraid, he may act aggressively or defensively. He may sleep more frequently because his daily walks, though shorter now, tire him out. He may begin to experience separation anxiety or, conversely, become less interested in petting and attention.

There also are clinical conditions that cause behavioral changes in older dogs. One such condition is known as canine cognitive dysfunction (familiarly known as "old-dog" syndrome). It can be frustrating for an owner whose dog is affected with cognitive dysfunction, as it can result in behavioral changes of all types, most seemingly unexplainable. Common changes include the dog's forgetting aspects of the daily routine, such as times to eat, go out for walks, relieve himself and the like. Along the same lines, you may take your dog out at the regular time for a potty trip and he may have no idea why he is there. Sometimes a placid dog will begin to show aggressive or possessive tendencies or, conversely, a hyperactive dog will start to "mellow out."

Disease also can be the cause of behavioral changes in senior dogs. Hormonal problems (Cushing's disease is common in older dogs), diabetes and thyroid

SHADY PINES? NOT YET

Is your "golden girl" ready for the "old dogs' home"? If your dog has retained his energy and is in good shape (not overweight), you should consider yourself lucky. An active older dog who enjoys his food should not be changed to a senior food just because he is "of age." One of the super premium adult foods (or even a growth or performance brand) might be a better choice for your feisty senior citizen. Every dog's condition and needs should be evaluated by his veterinarian. The correct diet for a senior provides the appropriate caloric density to maintain the body's condition as well as balanced nutrition.

disease can cause increased appetite, which can lead to aggression related to food guarding. It's better to be proactive with your senior dog, making more frequent trips to the vet if necessary and having bloodwork done to test for the diseases that can commonly befall older dogs.

This is not to say that, as dogs age, they all fall apart physically and become nasty in personality. The aforementioned changes are discussed to alert owners to the things that may happen as their dogs get older. Many hardy dogs remain active and alert well into old age. However, it can be frustrating and heartbreaking for owners to see their beloved dogs change physically and temperamentally. Just know that it's the same Border Collie under there, and that he still loves you and appreciates your care, which he needs now more than ever.

HOW DO I CARE FOR MY AGING DOG?

Again, every dog is an individual in terms of aging. Your dog might reach the estimated "senior" age of ten for Border Collies and show no signs of slowing down. However, even if he shows no outward signs of aging, he should begin a senior-care program once he reaches the determined age. He may not show it, but he's not a pup anymore! By providing him with extra attention to his veterinary care at this age, you will be practicing good preventive medicine, ensuring that the rest of your dog's life will be as long, active, happy and healthy as possible. If you do notice indications of aging, such as graying and/or changes in sleeping, eating or toileting habits, this is a sign to

WEATHER WORRIES
Older pets are less tolerant of extremes in weather, both heat and cold. Your older dog should not spend extended periods in the sun; when outdoors in the warm weather, make sure he does not become overheated. In chilly weather, consider a sweater for your dog when outdoors and limit time spent outside. Whether or not his coat is thinning, he will need provisions to keep him warm when the weather is cold. You may even place his bed by a heating duct in your living room or bedroom.

set up a senior-care visit with your vet right away to make sure that these changes are not related to any health problems.

To start, senior dogs should visit the vet twice yearly for exams, routine tests and overall evaluations. Many veterinarians have special screening programs especially for senior dogs that can include a thorough physical exam; blood test to determine complete blood count; serum biochemistry test, which screens for liver, kidney and blood problems as well as cancer; urinalysis; and dental exams. With these tests, it can be determined whether your dog has any health problems; the results also establish a baseline for your pet against which future test results can be compared.

In addition to these tests, your vet may suggest additional

testing, including an EKG, tests for glaucoma and other problems of the eye, chest X-rays, screening for tumors, blood pressure test, test for thyroid function and screening for parasites and reassessment of his preventive program. Your vet also will ask you questions about your dog's diet and activity level, what you feed and the amounts that you feed. This information, along with his evaluation of the dog's overall condition, will enable him to suggest proper dietary changes, if needed.

This may seem like quite a work-up for your pet, but veterinarians advise that older dogs need more frequent attention so that any health problems can be detected as early as possible. Serious conditions like kidney disease, heart disease and cancer may not present outward symptoms, or the problem may go undetected if the symptoms are mistaken by owners as just part of the aging process.

There are some conditions more common in elderly dogs that are difficult to ignore. Cognitive dysfunction shares much in common with senility and Alzheimer's disease, and dogs are not immune. Dogs can become confused and/or disoriented, lose their house-training, have abnormal sleep-wake cycles and interact differently with their owners. Be heartened by the fact that, in

some ways, there are more treatment options for dogs with cognitive dysfunction than for people with similar conditions. There is good evidence that continued stimulation in the form of games, play, training and exercise can help to maintain cognitive function. There are also medications (such as seligiline) and antioxidant-fortified senior diets that

The decision to replace a lost pet is a very personal one. When youngsters are involved, the new Border Collie pup will help fill the gap left by the deceased pet.

have been shown to be beneficial.

Cancer is also a condition more common in the elderly. Almost all of the cancers seen in people are also seen in pets. While we can't control the effects of second-hand smoke, lung cancer, which is a major killer in humans, is relatively rare in dogs. If pets are getting regular physical examinations, cancers are often detected early. There are a variety of cancer therapies available today, and many pets continue to live happy lives with appropriate treatment.

Degenerative joint disease, often referred to as arthritis, is another malady common to both elderly dogs and humans. A lifetime of wear and tear on joints and running around at play eventually take toll and result in stiffness and difficulty in getting around. As dogs live longer and healthier lives, it is natural that they should eventually feel some of the effects of aging. Once again, if regular veterinary care has been available, your pet was not carrying extra pounds all those years and wearing those joints out before their time. If your pet was unfortunate enough to inherit hip dysplasia, osteochondrosis dissecans, or any of the other developmental orthopedic diseases, battling the onset of degenerative joint disease was probably a long-standing goal. In any case, there are now many effective remedies for managing degenerative joint disease and a number of remarkable surgeries as well.

Aside from the extra veterinary care, there is much you can do at home to keep your older dog in good condition. The dog's diet is an important factor. If your dog's appetite decreases, he will not be getting the nutrients he needs. He also will lose weight, which is unhealthy for a dog at a proper weight. Conversely, an older dog's metabolism is slower and he usually exercises less, but he should not be allowed to become obese. Obesity in an older dog is especially risky, because

extra pounds mean extra stress on the body, increasing his vulnerability to heart disease. Additionally, the extra pounds make it harder for the dog to move about.

You should discuss age-related feeding changes with your vet. For a dog who has lost interest in food, it may be suggested to try some different types of food until you find something new that the dog likes. For an obese dog, a "light" formula dog food or reducing food portions may be advised,

CAUSES OF CHANGE

Cognitive dysfunction may not be the cause of all changes in your older dog; illness and medication can also affect him. Things like diabetes, Cushing's disease, cancer and brain tumors are serious physical problems but can cause behavioral changes as well. Older dogs are more prone to these conditions, which should not be overlooked as possibilities for your dog's acting not like his "old self." Any significant changes in your senior's behavior are good reasons to take your dog to the vet for a thorough exam.

Your dog's reactions to medication can cause changes as well. The various types of corticosteroids are often cited as affecting a dog's behavior. If your vet prescribes any type of drug, discuss possible side effects before administering the medication to your dog.

along with exercise appropriate to his physical condition and energy level.

As for exercise, the senior dog should not be allowed to become a "couch potato" despite his old age. He may not be able to handle the morning run, long walks and vigorous games of fetch, but he still needs to get up and get moving. Keep up with your daily walks, but keep the distances shorter and let your dog set the pace. If he gets to the point where he's not up for walks, let him stroll around the yard. On the other hand, many dogs remain very active in their senior years, so base changes to the exercise program on your own individual dog and what he's capable of. Don't worry, your Border Collie will let you know when it's time to rest.

Keep up with your grooming routine as you always have. Be extra diligent about checking the skin and coat for problems. Older dogs can experience thinning coats as a normal aging process, but they can also lose hair as a result of medical problems. Some thinning is normal, but patches of baldness or the loss of significant amounts of hair is not.

Hopefully, you've been regular with brushing your dog's teeth throughout his life. Healthy teeth directly affect overall good health. We already know that bacteria from gum infections can enter the

The Border Collie will return your good care, responsible ownership and friendship tenfold. You owe it to your canine friend to give him the best you can.

dog's body through the damaged gums and travel to the organs. At a stage in life when his organs don't function as well as they used to, you don't want anything to put additional strain on them. Clean teeth also contribute to a healthy immune system. Offering the dental-type chews in addition to toothbrushing can help, as they remove plaque and tartar as the dog chews.

Along with the same good care you've given him all of his life, pay a little extra attention to your dog in his senior years and keep up with twice-yearly trips to the vet. The sooner a problem is uncovered, the greater the chances of a full recovery.

AMERICAN KENNEL CLUB TITLES

The AKC offers over 50 different titles to dogs in competition. Depending on the events that your dog can enter, different titles apply. Some titles can be applied as prefixes, meaning that they are placed before the dog's name (e.g., Ch. King of the Road) and others are used as suffixes, placed after the dog's name (e.g., King of the Road, CD).

These titles are used as prefixes:

Conformation Dog Shows
- Ch. (Champion)

Obedience Trials
- NOC (National Obedience Champion)
- OTCH (Obedience Trial Champion)
- VCCH (Versatile Companion Champion)

Tracking Tests
- CT [Champion Tracker (TD,TDX and VST)]

Agility Trials
- MACH (Master Agility Champion)
- MACH2, MACH3, MACH4, etc.

Field Trials
- FC (Field Champion)
- AFC (Amateur Field Champion)
- NFC (National Field Champion)
- NAFC (National Amateur Field Champion)
- NOGDC (National Open Gun Dog Champion)
- AKC GDSC (AKC Gun Dog Stake Champion)
- AKC RGDSC (AKC Retrieving Gun Dog Stake Champion)

Herding Trials
- HC (Herding Champion)

Dual
- DC (Dual Champion — Ch. and FC)

Triple
- TC (Triple Champion — Ch., FC and OTCH)

Coonhounds
- NCH (Nite Champion)
- GNCH (Grand Nite Champion)
- SGNCH (Senior Grand Nite Champion)
- SGCH (Senior Grand Champion)
- GFC (Grand Field Champion)
- SGFC (Senior Grand Field Champion)
- WCH (Water Race Champion)
- GWCH (Water Race Grand Champion)
- SGWCH (Senior Grand Water Race Champion)

These titles are used as suffixes:

Obedience
- CD (Companion Dog)
- CDX (Companion Dog Excellent)
- UD (Utility Dog)
- UDX (Utility Dog Excellent)
- VCD1 (Versatile Companion Dog 1)
- VCD2 (Versatile Companion Dog 2)
- VCD3 (Versatile Companion Dog 3)
- VCD4 (Versatile Companion Dog 4)

Tracking Tests
- TD (Tracking Dog)
- TDX (Tracking Dog Excellent)
- VST (Variable Surface Tracker)

Agility Trials*
- NA (Novice Agility)
- OA (Open Agility)
- AX (Agility Excellent)
- MX (Master Agility Excellent)
- NAJ (Novice Jumpers with weaves)
- OAJ (Open Jumpers with weaves)
- AXJ (Excellent Jumpers with weaves)
- MXJ (Master Excellent Jumpers with weaves)

Hunting Test
- JH (Junior Hunter)
- SH (Senior Hunter)
- MH (Master Hunter)

Herding Test
- HT (Herding Tested)
- PT (Pre-Trial Tested)
- HS (Herding Started)
- HI (Herding Intermediate)
- HX (Herding Excellent)

Lure Coursing
- JC (Junior Courser)
- SC (Senior Courser)
- MC (Master Courser)

Earthdog
- JE (Junior Earthdog)
- SE (Senior Earthdog)
- ME (Master Earthdog)

*All titles also offered in Preferred Classes

BORDER COLLIE

Is dog showing in your blood? Are you excited by the idea of gaiting your handsome Border Collie around the ring to the thunderous applause of an enthusiastic audience? Are you certain that your beloved Border Collie is flawless? You are not alone! Every loving owner thinks that his dog has no faults, or too few to mention. No matter how many times an owner reads the breed standard, he cannot find any faults in his aristocratic companion dog. If this sounds like you, and if you are considering entering your Border Collie in a dog show, here are some basic questions to ask yourself:

- Did you purchase a "show-quality" puppy from the breeder?
- Is your puppy at least six months of age?

- Does the puppy exhibit correct show type for his breed?
- Does your puppy have any disqualifying faults?

While the Border Collie's favorite forum may be the herding trial, many handsome dogs excel in the show ring. This is a happy day for this winning duo.

- Is your Border Collie registered with the American Kennel Club?
- How much time do you have to devote to training, grooming, conditioning and exhibiting your dog?
- Do you understand the rules and regulations of a dog show?
- Do you have time to learn how to show your dog properly?

AKC GROUPS

For showing purposes, the American Kennel Club divides its recognized breeds into seven groups: Sporting Dogs, Hounds, Working Dogs, Terriers, Toys, Non-Sporting Dogs and Herding Dogs.

- Do you have the financial resources to invest in showing your dog?
- Will you show the dog yourself or hire a professional handler?
- Do you have a vehicle that can accommodate your weekend trips to the dog shows?

Success in the show ring requires more than a pretty face, a waggy tail and a pocketful of liver. Even though dog shows can be exciting and enjoyable, the sport of conformation makes great demands on the exhibitors and the dogs. Winning exhibitors live for their dogs, devoting time and money to their dogs' presentation, conditioning and training. Very few novices, even those with good dogs, will find themselves in the winners' circle,

BECOMING A CHAMPION

An official AKC championship of record requires that a dog accumulate 15 points under three different judges, including two "majors" under different judges. Points are awarded based on the number of dogs entered into competition, varying from breed to breed and place to place. A win of three, four or five points is considered a "major." The AKC annually assigns a schedule of points to adjust for variations that accompany a breed's popularity and the population of a given area.

though it does happen. Don't be disheartened, though. Every exhibitor began as a novice and worked his way up to the Group ring. It's the "working your way up" part that you must keep in mind.

Assuming that you have purchased a puppy of the correct type and quality for showing, let's begin to examine the world of showing and what's required to get started. Although the entry fee into a dog show is nominal, there are lots of other hidden costs involved with "finishing" your Border Collie, that is, making him a champion. Things like equipment, travel, training and conditioning all cost money. A more serious campaign will include fees for a professional handler, boarding, cross-country travel and advertising. Top-winning show dogs can represent a very considerable investment—over $100,000 has been spent in campaigning some dogs. (The investment can be less, of course, for owners who don't use professional handlers.)

Many owners, on the other hand, enter their "average" Border Collies in dog shows for the fun and enjoyment of it. Dog showing makes an absorbing hobby, with many rewards for dogs and owners alike. If you're having fun, meeting other people who share your interests and enjoying the overall experience, you likely will catch the "bug."

Once the dog-show bug bites, its effects can last a lifetime; it's certainly much better than a deer tick! Soon you will be envisioning yourself in the center ring at the Westminster Kennel Club Dog Show in New York City, competing for the prestigious Best in Show cup. This magical dog show is televised annually from Madison Square Garden, and the victorious dog becomes a celebrity overnight.

During the show, treats are often used to capture the dog's attention.

AMERICA'S ALTERNATIVE: THE UNITED KENNEL CLUB

The United Kennel Club defines itself as follows: "With 250,000 registrations annually, the United Kennel Club is the second oldest and second largest all-breed dog registry in the United States. Founded in 1898 by Chauncey Z. Bennett, the registry has always supported the idea of the 'total dog,' meaning a dog that looks and performs equally well. The performance programs of UKC include Conformation Shows, Obedience Trials, Agility Trials, Coonhound Field Trials, Water Races, Nite Hunts and Bench Shows, hunting tests for the retrieving breeds, beagle events including Hunts and Bench Shows, and, for Cur and Feist, Squirrel and Coon Events, and Bench Shows. Essentially, the UKC world of dogs is a working world. That's the way founder Chauncey Bennett designed it, and that's the way it remains today."

AKC CONFORMATION SHOWING

GETTING STARTED

Visiting a dog show as a spectator is a great place to start. Pick up the show catalog to find out what time your breed is being shown, who is judging the breed and in which ring the classes will be held. To start, Border Collies compete against other Border Collies, and the winner is selected as Best of Breed by the judge. This is the procedure for each breed. At a group show, all of the Best of Breed winners go on to compete for Group One in their respective group. For example, all Best of Breed winners in a given group compete against each other; this is done for all seven groups. Finally, all seven group winners go head to head in the ring for the Best in Show award.

What most spectators don't understand is the basic idea of conformation. A dog show is often referred as a "conformation" show. This means that the judge should decide how each dog stacks up (conforms) to the breed standard for his given breed: how well does this Border Collie conform to the ideal representative detailed in the standard? Ideally, this is what happens. In reality, however, this ideal often gets slighted as the judge compares Border Collie #1 to Border Collie #2. Again, the ideal is that each dog is judged based on his merits in comparison to his breed standard, not in comparison to the other dogs in the ring. It is easier for judges to compare dogs of the same breed to decide which they think is the better specimen; in the Group and Best in Show ring, however, it is very difficult to compare one breed to another, like apples to oranges. Thus the dog's conformation to the breed standard—not to mention advertising dollars and good handling—is essential to success in conformation shows. The dog described in the standard (the standard for each AKC breed is written and approved by the breed's national parent club and then submitted to the AKC for approval) is the perfect dog of that breed, and breeders keep their eye on the standard when they choose which dogs to breed, hoping to get closer and closer to the ideal with each litter.

More and more Border Collies compete in dog shows nationwide. A dog show is also called a conformation show, based on the principle that the dog that most closely *conforms* to the breed standard is the winner of the class.

Another good first step for the novice is to join a dog club. You will be astonished by the many and different kinds of dog clubs in the country, with about 5,000 clubs holding events every year. Most clubs require that prospective new members present two letters of recommendation from existing members. Perhaps you've made some friends visiting a show held by a particular club and you would like to join that club. Dog clubs may specialize in a single breed, like a local or regional Border Collie club, or in a specific pursuit, such as obedience, tracking or herding tests. There are all-breed clubs for all-dog enthusiasts; they sponsor special training days, seminars on topics like grooming or handling or lectures on breeding or canine genetics. There are also clubs that specialize in certain types of dogs, like herding dogs, hunting dogs, companion dogs, etc.

A parent club is the national organization, sanctioned by the AKC, which promotes and safeguards its breed in the country. The Border Collie and its many parent clubs paint a very modern family portrait. The breed has no fewer than three parent clubs, with the American Border Collie Association (ABCA) serving as its AKC club. The parent club holds an annual national specialty show, usually in a different state each year, in which many of the country's top dogs, handlers and breeders gather to compete. At a specialty show, only members of a single breed are invited to participate. There are also Group specialties, in which all members of a Group are invited. For more information about dog clubs in your area, contact the AKC at www.akc.org on the Internet or write them at their Raleigh, NC address.

CLASSES AT UNITED KENNEL CLUB DOG SHOWS

The Regular classes, for all dogs who are not Champions or Grand Champions, are divided by sex (and variety) with four winners selected by the judge. Champions and Grand Champions are judged separately, with one winner in each class. The Regular classes are broken down into the following:

Puppy Class: Male and female puppies, from six months to one year of age.

Junior Class: Male and female dogs, from one year to under two years of age.

Senior Class: Male and female dogs, from two years of age to under three years of age.

Adult Class: Male and female dogs, three years of age and older.

Breeder/Handler Class: Male and female dogs, six months of age and older, handled by the breeder of record or a member of the breeder's immediate family.

How Shows Are Organized

Three kinds of conformation shows are offered by the AKC. There is the all-breed show, in which all AKC-recognized breeds can compete; the specialty show, which is for one breed only and usually sponsored by the breed's parent club, and the group show, for all breeds in one of the seven AKC groups. The Border Collie competes in the Herding Group.

For a dog to become an AKC champion of record, the dog must earn 15 points at shows. The points must be awarded by at least three different judges and must include two "majors" under different judges. A "major" is a three-, four- or five-point win, and the number of points per win is determined by the number of dogs competing in the show on that day. (Dogs that are absent or are excused are not counted.) The number of points that are awarded varies from breed to breed. More dogs are needed to attain a major in more popular breeds, and fewer dogs are needed in less popular breeds. Yearly, the AKC evaluates the number of dogs in competition in each division (there are 14 divisions in all, based on geography) and may or may not change the numbers of dogs required for each number of points. For example, a major in Division 2 (Delaware, New Jersey and Pennsylvania) recently required 17 dogs or 16 bitches for a three-

point major, 29 dogs or 27 bitches for a four-point major and 51 dogs or 46 bitches for a five-point major. The Border Collie attracts numerically proportionate representation at all-breed shows.

Only one dog and one bitch of each breed can win points at a given show. There are no "co-ed" classes except for champions of record. Dogs and bitches do not compete against each other until they are champions. Dogs that are not champions (referred to as "class dogs") compete in one of five classes. The class in which a dog is entered depends on age and previous show wins.

> ## FIVE CLASSES AT SHOWS
>
> At most AKC all-breed shows, there are five regular classes offered: Puppy, Novice, Bred-by-Exhibitor, American-bred and Open. The Puppy Class is usually divided as 6 to 9 months of age and 9 to 12 months of age. When deciding in which class to enter your dog, whether male or female, you must carefully check the show schedule to make sure that you have selected the right class. Depending on the age of the dog, its previous first-place wins and the sex of the dog, you must make the best choice. It is possible to enter a one-year-old dog who has not won sufficient first places in any of the non-Puppy Classes, though the competition is more intense the further you progress from the Puppy Class.

The judge at the show begins judging the male dogs in the Puppy Class(es) and proceeds through the other classes. The judge awards first through fourth place in each class. The first-place winners of each class then compete with one another in the Winners Class to determine Winners Dog. The judge then starts over with the bitches, beginning with the Puppy Class(es) and proceeding up to the Winners Class to award Winners Bitch, just as he did with the dogs. A Reserve Winners Dog and Reserve Winners Bitch are also selected; they could be awarded the points in the case of a disqualification.

The Winners Dog and Winners Bitch are the two that are awarded the points for their breed. They then go on to compete with any champions of record (often called "specials") of their breed that are entered in the show. The champions may be dogs or bitches; in this class, all are shown together. The judge reviews the Winners Dog and Winners Bitch along with all of the champions to select the Best of Breed winner. The Best of Winners is selected between the Winners Dog and Winners Bitch; if one of these two is selected Best of Breed as well, he or she is automatically determined Best of Winners. Lastly, the judge selects Best of Opposite Sex to the Best of Breed winner. The Best of Breed

SHOW POTENTIAL

How possible is it to predict how your ten-week-old puppy will eventually do in the show ring? Most show dogs reach their prime at around three years of age, when their bodies are physically mature and their coats are in "full bloom." Experienced breeders, having watched countless pups grow into Best of Breed winners, recognize the glowing attributes that spell "show potential." When selecting a puppy for show, it's best to trust the breeder to recommend which puppy will best suit your aspirations. Some breeders recommend starting with a male puppy, which likely will be more "typey" than his female counterpart.

Few breeds excel at agility trials like the Border Collie. Agility trials are among the most popular events for Border Collies and their owners.

winner then goes on to the Group competition.

At a Group or all-breed show, the Best of Breed winners from each breed are divided into their respective groups to compete against one another for Group One through Group Four. Group One (first place) is awarded to the dog that best lives up to the ideal for his breed as described in the standard. A Group judge, therefore, must have a thorough working knowledge of many breed standards. After placements have been made in each Group, the seven Group One winners (from the Sporting Group, Toy Group, Hound Group, etc.) compete

against each other for the top honor, Best in Show.

OTHER TYPES OF COMPETITION

In addition to conformation shows, the AKC holds a variety of other competitive events. Obedience trials, agility trials and tracking trials are open to all breeds, while hunting tests, field trials, lure coursing, herding tests and trials, earthdog tests and coonhound events are limited to specific breeds or groups of breeds. The Junior Showmanship program is offered to aspiring young handlers and their dogs, and the Canine Good Citizen®

program is an all-around good-behavior test open to all dogs, pure-bred and mixed.

OBEDIENCE TRIALS

Mrs. Helen Whitehouse Walker, a Standard Poodle fancier, can be credited with introducing obedience trials to the United States. In the 1930s she designed a series of exercises based on those of the Associated Sheep, Police, Army Dog Society of Great Britain. These exercises were intended to evaluate the working relationship between dog and owner. Since those early days of the sport in the US, obedience trials have grown more and more popular, and now more than 2,000 trials each year attract over 100,000 dogs and their owners. Any dog registered with the AKC, regardless of neutering or other disqualifications that would preclude entry in conformation competition, can participate in obedience trials.

There are three levels of difficulty in obedience competition. The first (and easiest) level is the Novice, in which dogs can earn the Companion Dog (CD) title. The intermediate level is the Open level, in which the Companion Dog Excellent (CDX) title is awarded. The advanced level is the Utility level, in which dogs compete for the Utility Dog (UD) title. Classes at each level are further divided into "A" and "B,"

with "A" for beginners and "B" for those with more experience. In order to win a title at a given level, a dog must earn three "legs." A "leg" is accomplished when a dog scores 170 or higher (200 is a perfect score). The scoring system gets a little trickier when you understand that a dog must score more than 50% of the points available for each exercise in order to actually earn the points. Available points for each exercise range between 20 and 40.

A dog must complete different exercises at each level of obedience. The Novice exercises are the easiest, with the Open and finally

Training a Border Collie to jump on an obstacle course requires a great deal of equipment, time and patience.

Agility trials in the US are dominated by Border Collies; these three photographs convey but an inkling of the Border Collie's incomparable maneuverability

the Utility levels progressing in difficulty. Examples of Novice exercises are on- and off-lead heeling, a figure-8 pattern, performing a recall (or come), long sit and long down and standing for examination. In the Open level, the Novice-level exercises are required again, but this time without a leash and for longer durations. In addition, the dog must clear a broad jump, retrieve over a jump and drop on recall. In the Utility level, the exercises are quite difficult, including executing basic commands based on hand signals, following a complex heeling pattern, locating articles based on scent discrimination and completing jumps at the handler's direction.

Once he's earned the UD title, a dog can go on to win the prestigious title of Utility Dog Excellent (UDX) by winning "legs" in ten shows. Additionally, Utility Dogs who win "legs" in Open B and Utility B earn points toward the lofty title of Obedience Trial Champion (OTCh.). Established in 1977 by the AKC, this title requires a dog to earn 100 points as well as three first places in a combination of Open B and Utility B classes under three different judges. The "brass ring" of obedience competition is the AKC's National Obedience Invitational. This is an exclusive competition for only the cream of the obedience crop. In order to

Running a weave course, weaving in and out of upright stakes, is one of the events at agility trials. Winning requires the fastest and most flawless performance.

qualify for the invitational, a dog must be ranked in either the top 25 all-breeds in obedience or in the top three for his breed in obedience. The title at stake here is that of National Obedience Champion (NOC).

AGILITY TRIALS

Agility trials became sanctioned by the AKC in August 1994, when the first licensed agility trials were held. Since that time, agility certainly has grown in popularity by leaps and bounds, literally! The AKC allows all registered breeds (including Miscellaneous Class breeds) to participate, providing the dog is 12 months of age or older. Agility is designed so that the handler demonstrates

how well the dog can work at his side. The handler directs his dog through, over, under and around an obstacle course that includes jumps, tires, the dog walk, weave poles, pipe tunnels, collapsed tunnels and more. While working his way through the course, the dog must keep one eye and ear on the handler and the rest of his body on the course. The handler

Going through a collapsed tunnel is a difficult obstacle for many dogs, but this Border Collie handled the task gleefully.

Tending sheep is what Border Collies are all about. Sheepdog trials take advantage of the dogs' natural desire to work livestock.

runs along with the dog, giving verbal and hand signals to guide the dog through the course.

The first organization to promote agility trials in the US was the United States Dog Agility Association, Inc. (USDAA). Established in 1986, the USDAA sparked the formation of many member clubs around the country. To participate in USDAA trials, dogs must be at least 18 months of age.

The USDAA and AKC both offer titles to winning dogs, although the exercises and requirements of the two organizations differ. Agility Dog (AD), Advanced Agility Dog (AAD) and Master Agility Dog (MAD) are the titles offered by the USDAA, while the AKC offers Novice Agility (NA), Open Agility (OA), Agility Excellent (AX) and Master Agility Excellent (MX). Beyond these four AKC titles, dogs can

Sheepdog trials, more intense than AKC herding trials, require that a Border Collie fetch the sheep through a gate, steer them around a handler, drive them away from an obstacle, direct them into a pen, and then run them off the course.

time your dog jumps through the hoop—and you'll be having just as much (if not more) fun!

HERDING EVENTS

The first recorded sheepdog trial was held in Wales in the late 19th century; since then, the popularity of herding events has grown around the world. The AKC began offering herding events in 1989, and participation is open to all breeds in the Herding Group as well as Rottweilers and Samoyeds. These events are designed to evaluate the dogs' herding instincts, and the aim is to develop these innate skills and show that herding dogs today can still perform the functions for which they were originally intended, whether or not they are actually used in working capacities. Herding events are designed to simulate farm

win additional titles in "jumper" classes: Jumper with Weave Novice (NAJ), Open (OAJ) and Excellent (MXJ). The ultimate title in AKC agility is MACH, Master Agility Champion. Dogs can continue to add number designations to the MACH title, indicating how many times the dog has met the title's requirements (MACH1, MACH2 and so on).

Agility trials are a great way to keep your dog active, and they will keep you running, too! You should join a local agility club to learn more about the sport. These clubs offer sessions in which you can introduce your dog to the various obstacles as well as training classes to prepare him for competition. In no time, your dog will be climbing A-frames, crossing the dog walk and flying over hurdles, all with you right beside him. Your heart will leap every

Border Collies love working with sheep farmers...and the feeling is mutual. Herding trials are based on the dogs love for moving livestock.

situations and are held on two levels: tests and trials.

AKC herding tests are more basic and are scored on a pass/fail system, meaning that dogs do not compete against each other to earn titles. Titles at this level are the most basic Herding Tested (HT) and the more difficult Pre-Trial Tested (PT). In addition, there is a non-competitive certification program, Herding Instinct Tested, which gives you a chance to evaluate the potential that your dog may have for herding. If your dog successfully passes this test, he receives a Herding Instinct Certificate, which makes him eligible to enter herding trials.

The more challenging herding trial level is competitive and requires more training and experience. There are three different courses (A, B and C, each with a different type of farm situation) with different types of livestock (cattle, sheep or ducks). There are three titles available on each course, Herding Started, Herding Intermediate and Herding Advanced, with each level being progressively more difficult. Handlers can choose the type of course and type of livestock for their dogs based on the breed's typical use. Once a Herding Advanced title has been earned on a course, the dog can then begin to strive for the Herding Champion title.

In addition to events held by the AKC, breed clubs often hold herding events for these breeds. Other specialty organizations hold trials that are open to all herding breeds; the way these events are structured and the titles that are awarded differ from those of the AKC. For example, the American Herding Breed Association (AHBA) allows any breed with herding in its ancestry to participate, as well as allowing mixed-breed herding dogs. To pass the Herding Instinct Test, the handler works with the dog at the shepherd's direction while the shepherd evaluates the dog's willingness to approach, move and round up the sheep while at the same time following the instructions of his handler.

At the competition level in AHBA events, dogs work with their handlers to move sheep up and down the field, through gates and into a pen, and also to hold the sheep without a pen, all while being timed. This is an amazing sight to see! A good dog working with the shepherd has to be the ultimate man-dog interaction. Rare breeds were often traditionally used for herding and, fortunately, the AHBA is more than happy to have rare breeds participate. Club members and spectators love to welcome some of these wonderful dogs that they have only read about but never seen.

BORDER COLLIE

You chose your dog because something clicked the minute you set eyes on him. Or perhaps it seemed that the dog selected you and that's what clinched the deal. Either way, you are now investing time and money in this dog, a true pal and an outstanding member of the family. Everything about him is perfect...well, almost perfect. Remember, he is a dog! For that matter, how does he think *you're* doing?

Some experts contend that the Border Collie possesses the intelligence of a five-year-old human child.

UNDERSTANDING THE CANINE MINDSET

For starters, you and your dog are on different wavelengths. Your dog is similar to a toddler in that both live in the present tense only. A dog's view of life is based primarily on cause and effect, which is similar to the old saying, "Nothing teaches a youngster to hang on like falling off the swing." If your dog stumbles down a flight of three steps, the next time he will try the Superman approach and fling himself off the top one!

Your dog makes connections based on the fact that he lives in the present, so when he is doing something and you interrupt to dispense praise or a correction, a connection, positive or negative, is made. To the dog, that's like one plus one equals two! In the same sense, it's also easy to see that when your timing is off, you will cause an incorrect connection. The one-plus-one way of thinking is why you must never scold a dog for behavior that took place an hour, 15 minutes or even 5 seconds ago. But it is also why, when your timing is perfect, you can teach him to do all kinds of

Training your Border Collie to bring you the newspaper every day is usually simple if the dog has learned the basic commands.

wonderful things—as soon as he has made that essential connection. What helps the process is his desire to please you and to have your approval.

There are behaviors we admire in dogs, such as friendliness and obedience, as well as those behaviors that cause problems to a varying degree. The dog owner who encounters minor behavioral problems is wise to solve them promptly or get professional help. Bad behaviors are not corrected by repeatedly shouting "No" or getting angry with the dog. Only the giving of praise and approval for good behavior lets your dog understand right from wrong. The longer a bad behavior is allowed to continue, the harder it is to overcome. A responsible breeder is often able to help. Each dog is unique, so try not to compare your dog's behavior with

your neighbor's dog or the one you had as a child.

Have your veterinarian check the dog to see whether a behavior problem could have a physical cause. An earache or toothache, for example, could be the reason for a dog to snap at you if you were to touch his head when putting on his leash. A sharp correction from you would only increase the behavior. When a physical basis is eliminated, and if the problem is not something you understand or can cope with, ask for the name of a behavioral specialist, preferably one who is familiar with the Border Collie. Be sure to keep the breeder informed of your progress.

Many things, such as environment and inherited traits, form the basic behavior of a dog, just as in humans. You also must factor into his temperament the purpose for which your dog was originally bred. The major obstacle lies in

ONE BITE TOO MANY

It's natural for puppies to bite in play, but you must teach your puppy that this is unacceptable in human circles. Relax your hand, say "No bite" and offer him a toy. An adolescent dog is testing his dominance and will bite as a way of disobeying you. If not stopped in puppyhood, you will end up with an adult dog that will bite aggressively. All adult biting should be considered serious and dealt with by a professional.

the dog's inability to explain his behavior to us in a way that we understand. The one thing you should not do is to give up and abandon your dog. Somewhere a misunderstanding has occurred but, with help and patient understanding on your part, you should be able to work out the majority of bothersome behaviors.

AGGRESSION

"Aggression" is a word that is often misunderstood and is sometimes even used to describe what is actually normal canine behavior. For example, it's normal for puppies to growl when playing tug-of-war. It's puppy talk. There are different forms of dog aggression, but all are degrees of dominance, indicating that the dog, not his master, is (or thinks he is) in control. When the dog feels that he (or his control of the situation) is threatened, he will respond. The extent of the aggressive behavior varies with individual dogs. It is not at all pleasant to see bared teeth or to hear your dog growl or snarl, but these are signs of behavior that, if left uncorrected, can become extremely dangerous. A word of warning here: never challenge an aggressive dog. He is unpredictable and therefore unreliable to approach.

Nothing gets a "hello" from strangers on the street quicker than walking a puppy, but people

Border Collies are generally not aggressive dogs, though every individual is different and must be handled as such.

should ask permission before petting your dog so you can tell him to sit in order to receive the admiring pats. If a hand comes down over the dog's head and he shrinks back, ask the person to bring their hand up, underneath the pup's chin. Now you're correcting strangers, too! But if you don't, it could make your dog afraid of strangers, which in turn can lead to fear-biting. Socialization prevents much aggression before it rears its ugly head.

The body language of an aggressive dog about to attack is clear. The dog will have a hard, steady stare. He will try to look as big as possible by standing stiff-legged, pushing out his chest, keeping his ears up and holding his tail up and steady. The hackles on his back will rise so that a ridge of hairs stands up. This posture may include the curled lip, snarl and/or growl, or he may

THE TOP-DOG TUG
When puppies play tug-of-war, the dominant pup wins. Children also play this kind of game but, for their own safety, must be prevented from ever engaging in this type of play with their dogs. Playing tug-of-war games can result in a dog's developing aggressive behavior. Don't be the cause of such behavior.

be silent. He looks, and definitely is, very dangerous.

This dominant posture is seen in dogs that are territorially aggressive. Deliverymen are constant victims of serious bites from such dogs. Territorial aggression is the reason you should never, ever, try to train a puppy to be a watchdog. It can escalate into this type of behavior over which you will have no control. All forms of aggression must be taken seriously and dealt with immediately. If signs of aggressive behavior continue, or grow worse, or if you are at all unsure about how to deal with your dog's behavior, get the help of a professional.

Uncontrolled aggression, sometimes called "irritable aggression," is not something for the pet owner to try to solve. If you cannot solve your dog's dangerous behavior with professional help, and you (quite rightly) do not wish to keep a canine time-bomb in your home, you will have some important decisions to make. Aggressive dogs often cannot be rehomed successfully, as they are dangerous and unreliable in their behavior. An aggressive dog should be dealt with only by someone who knows exactly the situation that he is getting into and has the experience, dedication and ideal living environment to attempt rehabilitating the dog, which often is not possible. In these cases, the dog ends up having to be humanely put down. Making a decision about euthanasia is not an easy undertaking for anyone, for any reason, but you cannot pass on to another home a dog that you know could cause harm.

A milder form of aggression is the dog's guarding anything that he perceives to be his—his food dish, his toys, his bed and/or his crate. This can be prevented if you take firm control from the start. The young puppy can and should be taught that his leader will share, but that certain rules apply. Guarding is mild aggression only in the beginning stages, and it will worsen and become dangerous if you let it.

Don't try to snatch anything away from your puppy. Bargain for the item in question so that you can positively reinforce him when he gives it up. Punishment only results in worsening any aggressive behavior.

Many dogs extend their guarding impulse toward items they've stolen. The dog figures, "If I have it, it's mine!" (Some ill-behaved kids have similar tendencies.) An angry confrontation will only increase the dog's aggression. (Have you ever watched a child have a tantrum?) Try a simple distraction first, such as tossing a toy or picking up his leash for a walk. If that doesn't work, the best way to handle the situation is with basic obedience. Show the dog a treat, followed by calm, almost slow-motion commands: "Come. Sit. Drop it. Good dog," and then hand over the cheese! That's one example of positive-reinforcement training.

Children can be bitten when they try to retrieve a stolen shoe or toy, so they need to know how to handle the dog or to let an adult do it. They may also be bitten as they run away from a dog, in either fear or play. The dog sees the child's running as reason for pursuit, and even a friendly young puppy will nip at the heels of a runaway.

DOMINANCE

Dogs are born with dominance skills, meaning that they can be quite clever in trying to get their way. The "follow-me" trot to the cookie jar is an example. The toy dropped in your lap says "Play with me." The leash delivered to you along with an excited look means "Take me for a walk." These are all good-natured dominant behaviors. Ask your dog to sit before agreeing to his request and you'll remain "top dog."

Teach the kids not to run away from a strange dog and when to stop overly exciting play with their own puppy.

Fear biting is yet another aggressive behavior. A fear biter gives many warning signals. The dog leans away from the approaching person (sometimes hiding behind his owner) with his ears and tail down, but not in submission. He may even shiver. His hackles are raised, his lips curled. When the person steps into the dog's "flight zone" (a circle of 1 to 3 feet surrounding the dog), he attacks. Because of the fear factor, he performs a rapid attack-and-retreat. Because it is directed at a person, vets are often the victims of this form of aggression. It is frightening, but discovering and eliminating the cause of the fright will help overcome the dog's need to bite. Early socialization again plays a strong role in the prevention of this behavior. Again, if you can't cope with it, get the help of an expert.

SEPARATION ANXIETY

Any behaviorist will tell you that separation anxiety is the most common problem about which pet owners complain. It is also one of the easiest to prevent. Unfortunately, a behaviorist usually is not consulted until the dog is a stressed-out, neurotic mess. At that stage, it is indeed a problem that requires the help of a professional.

Training the puppy to the fact that people in the house come and go is essential in order to avoid this anxiety. Leaving the puppy in his crate or a confined area while family members go in and out, and stay out for longer and longer periods of time, is the basic way to desensitize the pup to the family's frequent departures. If you are at home most of every day, make it a point to go out for at least an hour or two whenever possible.

How you leave is vital to the dog's reaction. Your dog is no fool. He knows the difference between sweats and business suits, jeans and dresses. He sees you pat your pocket to check for your wallet, open your briefcase, check that you have your cell phone or pick up the car keys. He knows from the hurry of the kids in the morning that they're off to school until afternoon. Lipstick? Aftershave

> **A HOUSE DIVIDED**
>
> A second pet can be a beneficial addition to your household, but it also can result in chaos. Just because you like both animals does not mean that they agree! Here are some tips for chaos prevention:
> - Kittens and puppies usually get along with older cats or dogs because they're submissive.
> - The male/female combination works better than two of the same sex, especially in dogs.
> - When squabbles arise between normally friendly dogs, let them settle it between themselves. Stay completely away. Eliminate jealousy by refraining from petting, treating or even talking to either dog.

lotion? Lunch boxes? Every move you make registers in his sensory perception and memory. Your puppy knows more about your departures than the FBI. You can't get away with a thing!

Before you got dressed, you checked the dog's water bowl and his supply of toys (including a long-lasting chew toy), and turned the radio on low. You will leave him in what he considers his "safe" area, not with total freedom of the house. If you've invested in child safety gates, you can be reasonably sure that he'll remain in the designated area. Don't give him access to a window where he can watch you leave the house. If you're leaving for an hour or two, just put him into his crate with a safe toy.

Now comes the test! You are ready to walk out the door. Do not give your Border Collie a big hug and a fond farewell. Do not drag out a long goodbye. Those are the very things that jump-start separation anxiety. Toss a biscuit into the dog's area, call out "So long, pooch" and close the door. You're gone. The chances are that the dog may bark a couple of times, or maybe whine once or twice, and then settle down to enjoy his biscuit and take a lovely nap, especially if you took him for a nice long walk after breakfast. As he grows up, the barks and whines will stop because it's an old routine, so why should he make the effort?

When you first brought home the puppy, the come-and-go routine was intermittent and constant. He was put into his crate with a tiny treat. You left (silently) and returned in 3 minutes, then 5, then 10, then 15, then half an hour, until finally you could leave without out a problem and be gone for 2 or 3 hours. If, at any time in the future, there's a "separation" problem, refresh his memory by going back to that basic training.

Now comes the next most important part—your return. Do not make a big production of coming home. "Hi, poochie" is as grand a greeting as he needs. When you've taken off your hat and coat,

tossed your briefcase on the hall table and glanced at the mail, and the dog has settled down from the excitement of seeing you "in person" from his confined area, then go and give him a warm, friendly greeting. A potty trip is needed and a walk would be appreciated, since he's been such a good dog.

MATTERS OF SEX

For whatever reasons, real or imagined, most people tend to have a preference in choosing between a male and female puppy. Some, but not all, of the undesirable traits attributed to the sex of the dog can be suppressed by early spaying or neutering. The major advantage, of course, is that a neutered male or a spayed female will not be adding to the overpopulation of dogs.

An unaltered male will mark territory by lifting his leg everywhere, leaving a few drops of urine indoors on your furniture and

If your Border Collie is a chewer, be sure that you give him chew toys that are strong and safe. Some stuffed toys may contain dyes that might be dangerous.

appliances, and outside on everything he passes. It is difficult to catch him in the act, because he leaves only a few drops each time, but it is very hard to eliminate the odor. Thus the cycle begins, because the odor will entice him to mark that spot again.

If you have bought a bitch with the intention of breeding her, be sure you know what you are getting into. She will go through one or two periods of estrus each year, each cycle lasting about three weeks. During those times she will have to be kept confined to protect your furniture and to protect her from being bred by a male other than the one you have selected. Breeding should never be undertaken to "show the kids the miracle of birth." Bitches can die giving birth, and the puppies may also die. The dam often exhibits what is called "maternal aggression" after the pups are born. Her intention is to protect her pups, but in fact she can be extremely vicious. Breeding should be left to the experienced breeders, who do so for the betterment of the breed and with much research and planning behind each mating.

Mounting is not unusual in dogs, male or female. Puppies do it to each other and adults do it regardless of sex, because it is not so much a sexual act as it is one of dominance. It becomes very annoying when the dog mounts your legs, the kids or the couch

Some Border Collies are so exuberant with play that they will jump up and frighten guests to your home.

cushions; in these and any other instances of mounting, he should be corrected. Touching sometimes stimulates the dog, so pulling the dog off by his collar or leash, together with a consistent and stern "Off!" command, usually eliminates the behavior.

CHEWING
All puppies chew. All dogs chew. This is a fact of life for canines, and sometimes you may think it's what your dog does best! A pup starts chewing when his first set of teeth erupts and continues throughout the teething period. Chewing gives the pup relief from

itchy gums and incoming teeth and, from that time on, he gets great satisfaction out of this normal, somewhat idle, canine activity. Providing safe chew toys is the best way to direct this behavior in an appropriate manner. Chew toys are available in all sizes, textures and flavors, but you must monitor the wear-and-tear inflicted on your pup's toys to be sure that the ones you've chosen are safe and remain in good condition.

Puppies cannot distinguish between a rawhide toy and a nice leather shoe or wallet. It's up to you to keep your possessions away from the dog and to keep your eye on the dog. There's a form of destruction caused by chewing that is not the dog's fault. Let's say you allow him on the sofa. One day he takes a rawhide bone up on the sofa and, in the course of chewing on the bone, takes up a bit of fabric. He continues to chew. Disaster! Now you've learned the lesson: Dogs with chew toys have to be either kept off furniture and carpets, carefully supervised or put into their confined areas for chew time.

The wooden legs of furniture are favorite objects for chewing. The first time, tell the dog "Leave it!" (or "No!") and offer him a chew toy as a substitute. But your clever dog may be hiding under

Although Border Collies normally do not dig too avidly, some dogs really like to get their paws dirty.

the chair and doing some silent destruction, which you may not notice until it's too late. In this case, it's time to try one of the foul-tasting products, made specifically to prevent destructive chewing, that is sprayed on the objects of your dog's chewing attention. These products also work to keep the dog away from plants, trash, etc. It's even a good way to stop the dog from "mouthing" or chewing on your hands or the leg of your pants. (Be sure to wash your hands after the mouthing lesson!) A little spray goes a long way.

DIGGING

Digging is another natural and normal doggy behavior. Wild canines dig to bury whatever food they can save for later to eat. (And you thought *we* invented the doggy bag!) Burying bones or toys is a primary cause to dig. Dogs also dig to get at interesting little underground creatures like moles

FEAR BITING

The remedy for the fear biter is in the hands of a professional trainer or behaviorist. This is not a behavior that the average pet owner should attempt to correct. However, there are things you should not do. Don't sympathize with him, don't pet him and don't, whatever you do, pick him up – you could be bitten in the process, which is even scarier if you bring him up near your face.

> ## QUIET DOWN!
>
> If your dog barks excessively, don't bark back. Yelling at him only encourages him to keep it up. Barking at the garbage truck makes perfect sense to the dog—that man is stealing your garbage! When the garbage truck leaves, that spells success to the dog: he has scared away the garbage man with his bark! Pick a command word, something like "Quiet" or "No Bark," to stop his barking. The second he stops, tell him "Good dog" and toss him a toy.

and mice. In the summer, they dig to get down to cool earth. In winter, they dig to get beneath the cold surface to warmer earth.

The solution to the last two is easy. In the summer, provide a bed that's up off the ground and placed in a shaded area. In winter, the dog should either be indoors to sleep or given an adequate insulated doghouse outdoors. To understand how natural and normal this is you have only to consider the Nordic breeds of sled dog who, at the end of the run, routinely dig a bed for themselves in the snow. It's the nesting instinct. How often have you seen your dog go round and round in circles, pawing at his blanket or bedding before flopping down to sleep?

Domesticated dogs also dig to escape, and that's a lot more dangerous than it is destructive. A dog that digs under the fence is the one that is hit by a car or becomes lost. A good fence to protect a digger should be set 10 to 12 inches below ground level, and every fence needs to be routinely checked for even the smallest openings that can become possible escape routes.

Catching your dog in the act of digging is the easiest way to stop it, because your dog will make the "one-plus-one" connection, but digging is too often a solitary occupation, something the lonely dog does out of boredom. Catch your young puppy in the act and put a stop to it before you have a yard full of craters. It is more difficult to stop if your dog sees you gardening. If you can dig, why can't he? Because you say so, that's why! Some dogs are excavation experts, and some dogs never dig. However, when it comes to any of these instinctive canine behaviors, never say "never."

JUMPING UP

Jumping up is a device of enthusiastic, attention-seeking puppies, but adult dogs often like to jump up as well, usually as a form of canine greeting. This is a controversial issue. Some owners wouldn't have it any other way! They encourage their dogs, and the owners and dogs alike enjoy the friendly physical contact. Some owners think that it's cute when it comes from a puppy, but not from an adult.

Conversely, there are those who consider jumping up to be one of the worst kinds of bad manners to be found in a dog. Among this group inevitably are bound to be some of your best friends. There are two situations in which your dog should be restrained from any and all jumping up. One is around children, especially young children and those who are not at ease with dogs. The other is when you are entertaining guests. No one who comes dressed up for a party wants to be groped by your dog, no matter how friendly his intentions or how clean his paws.

The answer to this one is relatively simple. If the dog has already started to jump up, the first command is "Off," followed immediately by "Sit." The dog must sit every time you are about to meet a friend on the street or when someone enters your home, be it child or adult. You may have

Keeping a Border Collie entertained and active will stimulate his mind and body. Boredom is a common cause of many destructive behaviors.

to ask people to ignore the dog for a few minutes in order to let his urge for an enthusiastic greeting subside. If your dog is too exuberant and won't sit still, you'll have to work harder by first telling him "Off" and then issuing the down-stay command. This requires more work on your part, because the down is a submissive position and your dog is only trying to be super-friendly. A small treat is expected when training for this particular down.

If you have a real pet peeve about a dog's jumping up, then disallow it from the day your puppy comes home. Jumping up is a subliminally taught human-to-dog greeting. Dogs don't greet each other in this way. It begins because your puppy is close to the ground and he's easier to pet and cuddle if he reaches up and you bend over to meet him halfway. If

FOUR ON THE FLOOR
You must discourage your dog from jumping up to get attention or for any other reason. To do so, bump the jumper gently with your hip as you turn away. "Four on the floor" requires praise. Once the dog sits on command, prevent him from attempting to jump again by asking him to sit-stay before petting him. Back away if he breaks the sit.

you won't like it later, don't start it when he is young, but do give lots of praise and affection for a good sit.

BARKING

Here's a big, noisy problem! Telling a dog he must never bark is like telling a child not to speak! Consider how confusing it must be to your dog that you are using your voice (which is your form of barking) to teach him when to bark and when not to! That is precisely the reason not to "bark back" when the dog's barking is annoying you (or your neighbors). Try to understand the scenario from the dog's viewpoint. He barks. You bark. He barks again, you bark again. This "conversation"can go on forever!

The first time your adorable little puppy said "Yip" or "Yap, you were ecstatic. His first word! You smiled, you told him how smart he was—and you allowed him to do it. So there's that one-plus-one thing again, because he will understand by your happy reaction that "Mr. Alpha loves it when I talk." Ignore his barking in the beginning, and allow it, but don't encourage barking during play. Instead, use the "put a toy in it" method to tone it down. Add a very soft "Quiet" as you hand off the toy. If the barking continues, stand up straight, fold your arms and turn your back on the dog. If he barks, you won't play, and you should follow the same rule for all undesirable behavior during play.

Dogs bark in reaction to sounds and sights. Another dog's bark, a person passing by or even just rustling leaves can set off a barker. If someone coming up your driveway or to your door provokes a barking frenzy, use the saturation method to stop it. Have several friends come and go every three or four minutes over as long a period of time as they can spare (it could take a couple of hours). Attach about a foot of rope to the dog's collar and have

CURES FOR COMMON BOREDOM

Dogs are social animals that need company. Lonely and tied-out dogs bark, hoping that someone will hear them. Prevent this from happening by never tying your dog out in the yard and always giving him the attention that he needs. If you don't, then don't blame the dog. Bored dogs will think up clever ways to overcome their boredom. Digging is a common diversion for a dog left alone outside for too long. The remedy is to bring him indoors or put a layer of crushed stone in his confined outdoor area. If you catch him in the act of "gardening," it requires immediate correction. Keep your dog safe by embedding the fencing a foot or more below ground level to foil a would-be escape artist.

very small treats handy. Each time a car pulls up or a person approaches, let the dog bark once (grab the rope if you need to physically restrain him), say "Okay, good dog," give him a treat and make him sit. "Okay" is the release command. It lets the dog know that he has alerted you and tells him that you are now in charge. That person leaves and the next arrives, and so on and so on until everyone—especially the dog—is bored and the barking has stopped. Don't forget to thank your friends. Your neighbors, by the way, may be more than willing to assist you in this parlor game.

Excessive barking outdoors is more difficult to keep in check because, when it happens, he is outside and you are probably inside. A few warning barks are fine, but use the same method to tell him when enough is enough. You will have to stay outside with him for that bit of training.

There is one more kind of vocalizing which is called "idiot barking" (from idiopathic, meaning of unknown cause). It is usually rhythmic or a timed series of barks. Put a stop to it immediately by calling the dog to come. This form of barking can drive neighbors crazy and commonly occurs when a dog is left outside at night or for long periods of time during the day. He is completely and thoroughly

MY ONE AND ONLY

Your dog's got you, so he may turn up his nose at other people or consider them interlopers. While you appreciate your dog's loyalty to you, you want him to make other friends as well. Provide familiar people with treats to offer in the palms of their hands if or when the dog approaches them. Don't push it with strangers. Let him warm up to others by encouraging him to show off with an obedience routine (tricks included). An appreciative audience may bring out the ham in him.

bored! A change of scenery may help, such as relocating him to a room indoors when he is used to being outside. A few new toys or different dog biscuits might be the solution. If he is left alone and no one can get home during the day, a noontime walk with a local dog-sitter would be the perfect solution.

INDEX

My Border Collie

PUT YOUR PUPPY'S FIRST PICTURE HERE

Dog's Name _____

Date _____ Photographer _____